STARTING PHOTOGRAPHY

Second Edition

Michael Langford

Photography Course Leader
Royal College of Art, London

Focal Press
An Imprint of Butterworth-Heinemann
Linacre House, Jordan Hill, Oxford OX2 8DP
A division of Reed Educational and Professional Publishing Ltd

 A member of the Reed Elsevier plc group

OXFORD   BOSTON   JOHANNESBURG
MELBOURNE   NEW DELHI   SINGAPORE

First published 1976
Second edition 1993
Reprinted 1994, 1997

British Library Cataloguing in Publication Data
Langford, Michael
    Starting Photography. — 2Rev.ed
    I. Title
    771

ISBN 0 240 51348 7

Library of Congress Cataloging in Publication Data
Langford, Michael John, 1933–
    Starting photography/Michael Langford. — 2nd ed.
    p.   cm.
    Includes index.
    Summary: Discusses technical and artistic aspects of photography
    such as camera operation, darkroom procedures, and picture
    composition.
    ISBN 0 240 51348 7
    1. Photography.   [1. Photography.]   I. Title.
    TR149.L35   1993
    771–dc20   93–17759
                                                              CIP

Composition by Genesis Typesetting, Laser Quay, Rochester, Kent
Manufactured in Spain by GZ Printek.

CONTENTS

Preface 5

Part One – How Photography Works

1 Camera principles 6
2 The 35mm camera 10
3 Choosing film 17

Part Two – Creative Use of Camera Controls

4 Shutter speed 20
5 Aperture and point of focus 24
6 How much exposure to give 28
7 Changing lens focal length 33
8 Using flash 38

Part Three – Elements of Picture Making

9 Seeing and photographing 45
10 Creating emphasis 50
11 Pattern and shape 55
12 Colour and mood 58
13 Texture 60

Part Four – Tackling Subjects

14 People 62
15 Places 66
16 Animals 70
17 Close-up subjects 72
18 Working to a theme 76

Part Five – Identifying Errors

19 Assessing results from the lab 78

Part Six – Experimental Images

20 Movement and abstraction 82
21 Using lens attachments 89
22 Combining two exposures 92
23 Manipulating prints 95

Part Seven – Using a Studio

24 Setting up 101
25 Controlling lighting 103

Part Eight – Black and White Processing and Printing

26 Processing a film 108
27 Contact Printing 114
28 Enlarging 120

Part Nine – Presenting Photographs

29 Finishing off 130
30 Assessing your photography 137
31 How photography is used 138

Appendices

A Roll and Sheet-film Cameras 144
B Using a Hand Meter 146
C Chemically Treating Black and White Prints 148
D Health and Safety in Photography 150

Glossary 151

How They Were Taken 155

Index 158

E000496/97 9001

Preface

This is a practical book for absolute beginners – amateurs with average 35mm cameras who send their films to the local lab for processing. It is also for young people at school taking photography as part of GCSE, and adults doing non-professional photography as a City and Guilds subject.

Much of the information here is provided visually, through colour and black and white photographs taken with ordinary cameras. Technical aspects concentrate on procedures that have a direct bearing on practical results. If you are about to buy a camera then reading this book will help you identify what features it should offer for the kinds of subject matter you intend to tackle.

Making photographs is interesting and challenging in all sorts of ways. It's a method of making pictures which does not demand that you be skilled at drawing; a way of showing and commenting on situations which does not insist that you be good at words. Nor is it necessary to have the latest, most expensive 'gee-whizz' camera to get telling shots.

What photography demands of you most is the ability to *observe* – really notice your surroundings, simple every-day objects, people in the world around you. Don't take these things for granted just because they are familiar. Develop your awareness of the way lighting and viewpoint alter appearances, and be quick thinking enough to sum up a situation or capture an expression by selecting the right moment to shoot.

You must also choose the most effective way to compose subjects in the picture area to emphasise important things, and suppress others. You need to take the right technical decisions to turn the scene in the viewfinder into a successful picture on paper. At every stage there is plenty of scope to produce photographs exploiting your own original ideas on subject matter, approach and execution.

Starting Photography begins with the camera itself, explaining key features – shutter, focus, flash, etc. – in terms of the creative options each one offers. Part Three, 'Elements of Picture Making' then looks at ways pictures might be structured to give them simplicity and strength, whatever your actual subject. Further sections suggest ways of approaching different kinds of subject; identification of faulty pictures in results from the lab; and ways of making unusual pictures without needing costly equipment.

Parts Seven and Eight show what is involved if you want to set up an indoor 'studio', or begin to process and print your own (black and white) pictures. Finally the book discusses ways of presenting and assessing your results, whether lab- or self-produced.

Although not primarily a school book, if you are working for GCSE you will find that *Starting Photography* (including Appendices and Glossary) covers most of the common core content and practical studies of the Southern Examining Group's syllabus for the National Curriculum. It is also applicable to City and Guilds 'Starting photography' and 'Black and White photography' modules. Above all the book is aimed at you as a beginner, with the hope that ideas and suggestions it contains encourage you to make fullest possible use of your camera.

Michael Langford

1.1 The basic principle – a simple lens forming an image on film.

PART ONE – HOW PHOTOGRAPHY WORKS

1 Camera principles

The word *Photography* means *drawing (or writing) with light*. It's a good description because every time you take a photograph you are really allowing light from the subject to draw its own picture on film. But just how does this 'automatic drawing' take place? Have you ever been lying in bed in the morning watching patterns formed on walls or ceiling by sunlight coming through gaps in the curtains? Sometimes the shadowy shapes of trees and buildings can be made out, especially if the curtains are dark with only one narrow space between them. If you can use a room with a window small enough, cover the window completely with black paper or opaque kitchen foil. Pierce a small clean hole through the black-out with a ball-point pen. Provided the daylight is fairly strong you should be able to see the dim outlines of the scene outside projected on a piece of thin paper held 30 cm (1 ft) or so from the hole (Figure 1.2). Various shapes should be visible, although everything will be upside down.

This arrangement for making images is called a *camera obscura*, meaning 'darkened chamber'. It has been known for centuries, and all sorts of portable camera obscuras like the one on page 8 were made which allowed people to trace over the image, and so help them draw scenes. Figure 1.3 shows a camera obscura you can make yourself out of an old cardboard cylinder and tracing paper. The image is

6

1.2 Using a pinhole in a blacked-out room to form an image of the garden on tracing paper

upside down because light always travels in straight lines. Light from the *top* of the window passing through the small hole reaches the *bottom* of the image on the paper.

Enlarging the hole makes the image brighter but much more blurred. However, you can greatly improve clarity *and* brightness by using a magnifying glass instead of just an empty hole. A magnifier is a piece of glass polished so that its edges are thinner than its centre. This forms a converging *lens* which is able to give a brighter and more detailed image of the scene. Try fitting a lens of this kind

1.3 Making a camera obscura

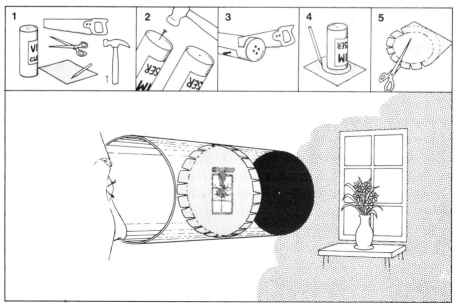

1.4 Portable camera obscura (1681) using a spectacle lens

1.5–9 A pinhole image (top left) is made up of circular patches of light. A lens (right) bends light and brings it to a point of sharp focus (F). It also passes more light, giving a brighter picture. Photographs (below) were taken with (left) pinhole; (centre) cheap magnifying glass; (right) camera lens

to your camera obscura, in place of the hole. You will find that you now need some way of altering the distance between lens and screen ('focusing') until the best position is found to give a clear, detailed image.

The three pictures below show how much image detail is improved when you use a properly made camera lens. Most camera lenses are made up of several lenses in a single housing. The faults, or 'aberrations', of the individual elements cancel out to give clearer, 'sharper' images.

We have now almost invented the photographic camera, but need some way of recording the image without actually having to trace it by hand. There are many materials which are sensitive to light. Curtains and carpets and paintwork of all kinds gradually fade under strong illumination. Newspaper yellows if left out in the sun. The trouble with these sorts of materials is that they are much too slow in their reaction – exposure times measured in years would be needed to record a visible picture in the camera. So instead we use chemical compounds of silver, which are extremely light-sensitive and

8

change from creamy colour to black. The silver compounds are mixed with gelatine and coated onto film, giving it a yellowish looking appearance called a 'light-sensitive emulsion'.

Scientists discovered too that it is not even necessary to wait until the silver darkens in the camera. You can just let the image light act on it for a fraction of a second, keep the film in the dark, and then later place it in a solution of chemicals which develops the silver until the recorded image is strong enough to be visible.

With most films processing gives us a *negative* picture on film. Subjects which were white appear as black metallic silver, and dark subjects as clear film. Parts of the subjects which were neither light nor dark are represented as intermediate silver density. The negative is then printed in the darkroom onto paper coated with a similar emulsion containing silver compounds. After development the image on the paper is 'a negative of the negative', i.e. the paper appears white where the original subject was light, black where it was dark and a suitable grey tone where it was in-between. We have a *positive* print. The advantage of using negative and positive stages is that many prints can be run off one camera exposure. And by putting the negative in an enlarger (which is rather like a slide projector) enlarged prints can be made. So you don't have to have a big camera to make big photographs.

The diagram, right, shows the main technical steps in making a black and white photograph. They also apply to colour photography, although different film and chemicals are needed.

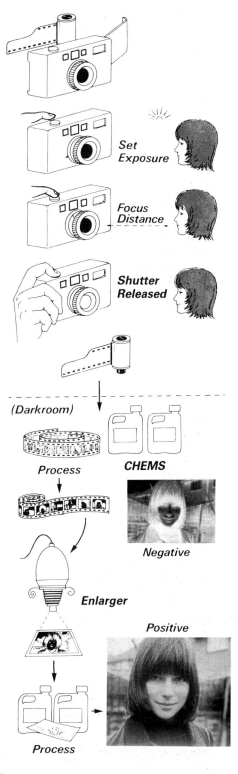

Set Exposure

Focus Distance

Shutter Released

(Darkroom)

Process   **CHEMS**

Negative

Enlarger

Positive

Process

1.10 (Right) The main stages in making a photograph – from loading and using the camera (top) to processing and printing the film (bottom)

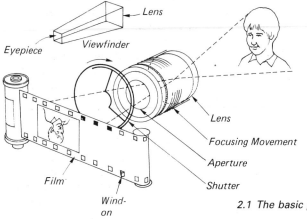

Eyepiece   Viewfinder   Lens

Lens

Focusing Movement

Aperture

Film

Shutter

Wind-on

2.1 The basic parts of a simple camera

2   The 35mm camera

There are so many cameras you can buy that to begin with it is quite confusing. Remember though, every camera is basically just a light-tight box with a lens at one end and light-sensitive film at the other. The photograph on page 6 shows what taking a picture would be like if the camera body was missing. Cameras vary a great deal in detail but they all possess the basic features shown above (Figure 2.1) in one form or another. These are firstly a lens positioned the correct focusing distance from the film; a shutter; a lens aperture; a viewfinder; a means of winding on the film, and a frame number indicator to show how many pictures you have taken.

The lens is the most important part of the whole camera. It must be protected from fingermarks and scratches, otherwise images resemble what you see when your eyes are watering. The spacing of the lens from the film has to change for subjects at different distances. Cheapest cameras have the lens 'fixed' to suit an average distance. Others have a ring or lever with a scale of distances (or symbols for 'groups', 'portraits' etc.). Operating this focusing control moves the lens slightly further from the film the nearer your

subject. Many cameras have lenses with an autofocusing mechanism able to alter focusing to suit the distance of whatever the camera is pointing at in the centre of your picture. In all cases subjects closer than the closest setting the camera allows will not appear sharp, unless you fit an extra close-up lens or extension ring (see page 73).

The shutter prevents light from the lens reaching the film until you press the release button, so it allows you to decide exactly when the picture will be taken. On simplest cameras it may function at one speed only, typically opening for about 1/60 second, although this may not be marked. Most shutters offer a range of ten or so speed settings, from whole seconds down to 1/250 second or less. The choice allows you to 'freeze' or 'blur' moving subjects, and also compensate for dim or bright lighting. On fully automatic cameras shutter speed is selected by the camera mechanism itself, mostly according to the light (see page 30).

The aperture (also known as the *diaphragm* or *stop*) is a circular hole positioned within or just behind the lens. It is usually adjustable in size – changing to a smaller or larger diameter makes the

10

image dimmer or brighter, so you can compensate for strong or weak lighting conditions. The shutter therefore controls the *time* the image is allowed to act on the film, and the aperture controls the *brightness* of the image. Together they allow you to control the total exposure to light the film receives. The aperture also has an important effect on whether parts of scenes closer and further away than the subject for which you focused also appear sharp. The smaller the aperture the greater this foreground-to-background sharpness or *'depth of field'* (see page 24).

Very basic cameras have one fixed aperture, or 2–3 settings simply marked in weather symbols. Most cameras offer half a dozen aperture settings which are given *'f-numbers'*. Each change of *f*-number lets in half, or double the light, explained further on page 25. Automatic cameras have an aperture setting selected by the camera mechanism in response to the brightness of your subject lighting.

The viewfinder allows you to aim the camera and preview how much of your subject will be included in the subject. Some cameras have a separate viewfinder window above the lens (Figure 2.3) and others, known as single lens reflex cameras, allow you to look inside the camera itself and view the image formed by the lens (Figure 2.6). For serious picture composition it is important that the view-finder shows you the whole scene clearly and accurately, whether you are shooting close or far away.

The wind-on. Cameras accepting 35 mm wide film in cassettes use a roller with teeth to engage in the film's two rows of perforations. Winding-on after each picture is taken moves the film onto a take-up spool (see page 12). At the same time a frame number, displayed in a window on the camera body, shows you how many shots you have taken.

Although all the features above are found in every camera the way they are presented to you to use (or arranged to function automatically) varies from one brand to another. Cameras fall into two main 'families': (1) Compact cameras, which have a viewfinder separated from the lens and tend to be all-in-one, with no add-on extras. (2) Single lens reflexes which allow you to see through the taking lens, and are often the nucleus of a kit comprising a whole range of interchangeable lenses and other attachments. Both are made in manual and automated forms.

Compact cameras

These are also called *'point & shoot'*, or *'direct viewfinder'* cameras because of the viewfinder window (with eyepiece at the back of the camera) which gives you a direct view of the subject. You see your subject clear and bright, and apparently with everything always in focus.

Simple compacts (Figure 2.3) are the cheapest of all cameras. Most settings are 'fixed', so all you have to do after loading the film is to point the camera, press the shutter, and wind on. This sounds ideal but since the lens is fixed to focus subjects about 15 ft away you cannot get sharp pictures closer than about 8 ft (the limit of depth of field). Nor can you take shots with foreground detail sharp and background unsharp. The fixed shutter speed of about 1/40 second is too slow to freeze fast movement, and also means you must hold the camera very still. The fixed (or limited range) aperture means that

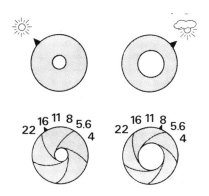

2.2 Aperture adjustment. Top: simple camera. Bottom: camera with f numbers. Set (left) for bright sun and (right) for cloudy weather

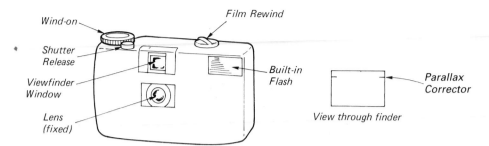

Wind-on

Film Rewind

Shutter
Release

Viewfinder
Window

Built-in
Flash

Lens
(fixed)

Parallax
Corrector

View through finder

2.3 A low cost, simple compact camera.
(Right) looking through the viewfinder
correction lines shows the top of your

picture with close subjects the lens is just
able to focus

you cannot adjust exposure for a wide range of lighting conditions, nor choose between deep or shallow depth of field (see page 24). The viewfinder, being an inch or so from the taking lens 'sees' your subject from a slightly different position. This difference of viewpoint or *parallax error* becomes greater the closer your subject.

Nevertheless, reasonable photographs can be taken with a simple compact (Figures 11.1 and 14.3 are both examples) provided you work within its limitations. Load fast (ISO 400) film for correct exposure in cloudy conditions, slow (ISO 100) film for bright sunshine, and use flash indoors. 'Disposable' cameras pre-loaded with fast film are also simple compacts, having fixed focus and no exposure controls.

Top-of-the-range compact cameras are much more expensive. They too present you with little or nothing to adjust but give technically good results over a wide range of lighting conditions and subject distances. They do this by electronic automation. For example, a camera as shown in Figure 2.5 will sense whether the film you have loaded is fast or slow in sensitivity, together with its length. A sensor behind a small window near the lens measures the brightness of your subject. The camera uses this film and subject information to set an appropriate aperture and shutter speed – ranging from smallest aperture and fastest speed in brilliant lighting, to widest aperture and slowest holdable speed in dim light.

Two further windows near the camera top sense the distance to whatever you have composed centrally in the view-finder. As you press the release button a

2.4 How to insert 35 mm film

MANUAL FILM LOADING

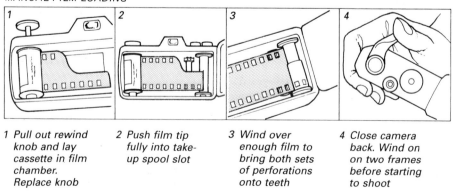

1 Pull out rewind
knob and lay
cassette in film
chamber.
Replace knob

2 Push film tip
fully into take-
up spool slot

3 Wind over
enough film to
bring both sets
of perforations
onto teeth

4 Close camera
back. Wind on
on two frames
before starting
to shoot

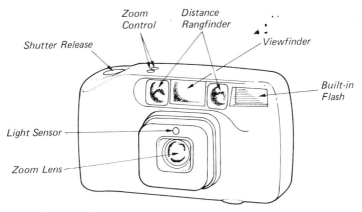

Shutter Release

Zoom Control

Distance Rangfinder

Viewfinder

Built-in Flash

Light Sensor

Zoom Lens

2.5 Fully automatic compact camera

motor adjusts the lens focus to suit this distance. If the subject is too close the camera signals a warning in the view-finder eyepiece; if lighting is too dim another signal warns you and may auto-matically switch on the flash. When the flash is in use it will automatically sense how much light to give out, according to subject distance and whether other light-ing is present too. After each shot a motor winds on one frame, and after the last picture on the film it winds it all back into the cassette ready to unload.

The only control offered, apart from shutter release, is a focal length changing 'zoom' button which makes the image bigger or smaller. This allows you to get more (or less) of a scene to fill your picture without having to move further

back (or closer) see page 33. The cam-era's viewfinder automatically adjusts to match focal length changes. It also tilts slightly according to the distance of your autofocused subject to compensate for parallax error and so more accurately show what you are getting in.

Between completely fixed and com-pletely automatic compact cameras you will find a whole range of compact cameras at intermediate prices. Some are cheaper because they omit completely one of the features described, such as a zoom lens; or they may not be fully automatic – expecting you to make some decisions, and settings, of your own. Having a camera with settable controls is often an advantage, as you will see from Chapter 4.

AUTOLOAD

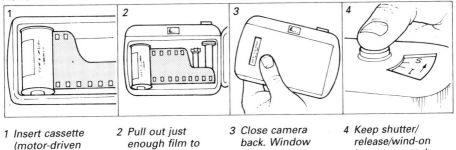

1 Insert cassette (motor-driven camera has no rewind knob)

2 Pull out just enough film to lay across and touch far end

3 Close camera back. Window allows you to read film data off cassette

4 Keep shutter/ release/wind-on button pressed until counter moves from S to 1.

Single lens reflex cameras (SLRs)

All SLR cameras have a clever optical system (as shown below) which allows you to view an image of the subject formed by the lens until just before exposing your picture. Unlike a compact camera, the shutter is not in the lens but in the back of the camera just in front of the film. Looking into an eyepiece at the back of an SLR you observe a small ground glass focusing screen, onto which the lens image is reflected by a mirror. So you see what the lens sees, and as the focusing control is turned it is easy to see exactly which parts of the subject are in focus. When you are satisfied that the picture is also correctly composed you press the release button. The mirror then rises out of the way, blocking out the focusing screen briefly and allowing the image to reach the back of the camera where the shutter opens to expose the film. As the distance from lens to film is the same as

lens to screen (via the mirror) what was focused on visually will also be in focus on the film, and there is no parallax error, however close the subject.

By having the shutter at the back you can remove the lens and fit others of different focal length, even mid-film. In fact single lens reflexes are 'system cameras' meaning that the makers offer a wide range of lenses of different kinds, plus adaptors to fit the camera body to microscopes or telescopes, attachments for ultra close working and so on. Starting off with a camera body and lens you can gradually build up quite an elaborate camera outfit bit-by-bit as you become more experienced.

The most basic SLR is a so-called 'manual' type (Figure 2.6). It costs about the equivalent of a mid price range compact. Having loaded the film and used the wind-on lever until '1' appears on the frame-counter you set your film's ISO speed number in a window. Next you look

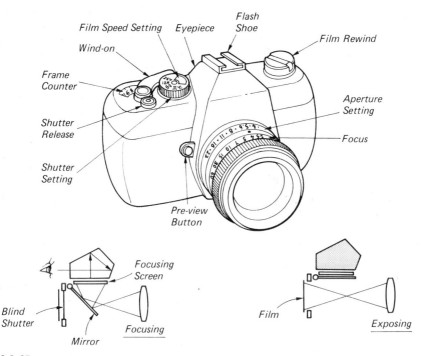

2.6 35mm manual-type SLR camera.
(Below) cross-section when (left)

composing and focusing, and (right)
exposing the picture

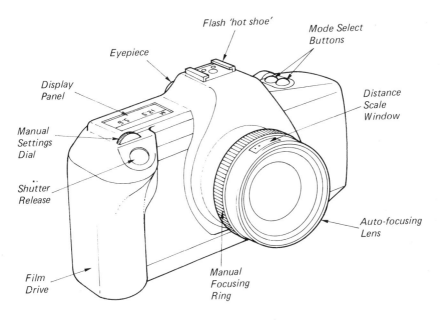

Flash 'hot shoe'

Mode Select
Buttons

Eyepiece

Display
Panel

Distance
Scale
Window

Manual
Settings
Dial

Shutter
Release

Auto-focusing
Lens

Film
Drive

Manual
Focusing
Ring

2.7 Advanced multi-mode SLR camera

through the eyepiece and turn the lens focusing ring until the most important part of your picture appears sharp. Typically you then set a shutter speed such as 1/125 second if you are hand-holding the camera (see page 20). Look through the eyepiece, half depress the shutter release and turn the aperture control until a signal light or needle next to the focusing screen indicates that the exposure set is correct. Alternatively you can first make an aperture setting because depth of field is important (see page 24) and then alter the *shutter* setting until correct exposure is signalled. Pressing fully on the release then takes your picture and you must wind-on to the next frame.

A manual SLR camera therefore requires you to know something about technical settings, but it will tackle a much wider range of lighting conditions and subject distances than all but the most advanced compacts. Since it makes minimal use of electronics it will still take photographs with the batteries flat. To use flash you attach a separate flashgun.

A top of the range electronic SLR (Figure 2.7) has autofocusing, motorized

film wind, and what is known as 'multi-mode' functioning. Multi-mode means that by selecting one mode you can have the camera function as if it were manual, or by selecting another have it totally autoprogrammed (just point and shoot). Yet another mode will allow you to choose and set shutter speed but makes every other setting automatically, whilst a fourth mode allows you to make the aperture your priority choice instead.

An advanced SLR camera like this offers you an almost overwhelming range of other options. They include shooting sequences of pictures at up to five per second. You can even programme the camera to take a rapid 'burst' of three pictures when you press the button, each one at slightly different exposure settings. As the shutter is electronically timed it offers a much wider setting range (typically 1/8000–30 seconds) than a manual camera shutter. Other mode settings, or slip-in logic cards, adjust the camera's auto-programme to best suit anticipated priorities when photographing 'action', or 'landscape' or 'portraits' (see pages 62–71).

All the information you need such as the chosen mode, shutter and aperture settings made, number of pictures left, etc., appears on a panel on top of the camera body. Some of this data is also displayed alongside the focusing screen when you look through the eyepiece.

Which camera is best?

There is no ideal camera, which is why so many variations exist even within the two types discussed here. (For other, non 35mm film cameras, see page 144.) Even if you buy the most expensive multi-mode electronic SLR having so many options available can be confusing, overwhelming your picture making. Just keeping it set to 'program' is wasteful if you then never use its other possibilities.

A fully automatic compact camera is quick to use and easy to carry. You can concentrate on composition, viewpoint and people's expressions when taking pictures, knowing that technicalities like focus and exposure are taken care of. On the other hand if you are unable to make individual settings – such as distance, shutter speed and aperture – you deprive yourself of many of the creative visual possibilities shown in Chapters 4–8. If you choose a low cost simple camera remember that poorly lit, fast moving

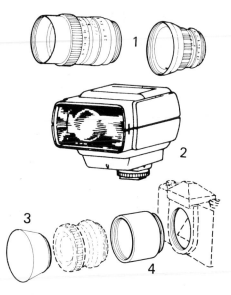

2.8 SLR accessories include different focal length lenses (1), clip-on flashgun (2), lens hood (3), and extension ring for close-ups (4)

close-up subjects (Figure 4.2, for example) will be beyond its capabilities. If you are prepared to learn to set the controls it is still difficult to beat a manual SLR. Such a camera accepts a great range of accessories, see above, including the same high quality lenses used on the most expensive SLR.

3 Choosing film

Film, 35mm wide and double perforated, comes in a light-tight cassette you load into your camera's empty film compartment (see Figure 2.4). The film's paler, light-sensitive surface faces the back of the lens. As you take pictures the film winds onto an open take-up spool within the camera. You therefore have to rewind it back safely into the cassette before opening the camera and removing your exposed film. Never load or remove film in bright light – especially direct sunlight. (The slot in the cassette through which the film protrudes has a velvet lining, but intense light may still penetrate.) Always find a shady area or at least turn away from the light.

The film box gives you all the important information. Apart from brand it shows the number of pictures, film speed, type, and the 'use by' date. Speed, length and type are also encoded in a chequerboard pattern on the side of the cassette (Figure 3.1). Most modern cameras contain four or six electrical contacts which press against this pattern and so programme the exposure measuring circuit for film speed, etc. The fewer contacts your camera contains the narrower the range of film speeds it will programme.
Number of pictures. The standard picture format given by a 35mm camera is 24 × 36 mm, and you can buy cassettes containing sufficient length of film for either 24 or 36 pictures. A few films are made in 12 exposure lengths. The longer the film, the cheaper per exposure.
Film 'speed'. Your film's light sensitivity is shown by its ISO (International Standards Organization) speed rating. A doubling of the ISO number means that a film is twice as sensitive or 'fast'. Films of about ISO 100 or less are regarded as 'slow' in speed, ISO 200 and 400 are 'medium', and 800 upwards 'fast'. Choose a fast film if all your pictures will be shot under dim lighting conditions with a simple camera, or you don't want to have to use a slow shutter speed or wide lens aperture. On the other hand the pattern of grains forming the image after processing is always coarser on fast film (colour or black and white). Sometimes 'graininess' suits a subject, like Figure 3.3. But since it destroys fine detail and coarsens tones it would not be best choice for the fine pattern and texture in Figure 3.4. Fast film is also more expensive.

A slow film suits bright light conditions where you don't want to be forced to keep using a fast shutter speed or small lens aperture. It's also the best choice if you plan to have a big enlargement made showing minimum grain pattern. For most other situations a medium speed

Chequerboard
DX Pattern

3.1 *A typical cassette of 35 mm film. The film's light-sensitive surface is shown facing you*

3.2

Typical Film Speeds Available:			
	B & W	Col Neg	Col Slide	
Slow	ISO 25–125	ISO 25–100	ISO 25–160	Fine Grain
Medium	400–800	200–400	200–400	Medium
Fast	1250–3200	1000–3200	640–1000	Coarse Grain

3.3 *Fast film produces coarse 'grain'*

film offers the best compromise. Always check that your camera is properly set for the ISO rating of the film it contains, every time you reload. Some compact cameras only offer settings for films between ISO 100 and 400.

Film type. Colour negative films are the most popular and there is the widest range of brands covering most ISO speeds. From colour negatives it is possible to have enlargements made cheaply in colour or (some labs) in black and white. Labs can also return your colour pictures on a CD ready for replay through a television set.

Black and white films make a refreshing change. Pictures are simplified into monochrome without the realism (and sometimes distraction) of colours. Few labs offer a black and white processing service, however. One solution is to use the type of monochrome negative film – Ilford XP2 for example – which labs can process in their regular colour chemicals and produce black and white results. Black and white is also your best choice to start your own processing and printing (see page 108).

Colour slide films are designed to be 'reversal' processed so that positive colour images are formed in the film instead of negatives. You can then project them as slides (see page 135). It is possible to have colour prints made off slides, although these are more expensive than off colour negatives. Again when shooting slides you must be more accurate with exposure than with negatives and, where necessary, have a filter to correct the lighting (see page 103). This is because there is no printing stage at which corrections can be made.

18

3.4 Slow film records finest detail

Expiry date. This is the 'use before' date on the film box. It assumes average storage conditions away from fumes, heat and humidity. Outdated film becomes less light sensitive, and colours may suffer. To extend shelf life store your films (sealed) in the main compartment of your refrigerator.

PART TWO – CREATIVE USE OF CAMERA CONTROLS

4 Shutter speed

Each camera feature, shutter, focus, aperture, focal length, flash, is there for two purposes. Firstly it helps you to get clear, well framed and properly exposed pictures of subjects – distant or close, under dim or bright lighting conditions. Each control also has its own particular effect on the image too. So you may choose a particular setting for its creative influence, and then adjust the other controls if necessary to maintain correct exposure. Clearly the more controls your camera offers and the wider their range the more choices you will be able to make.

Shutter speeds and movement

When using your camera hand-held a setting of $\frac{1}{125}$ second should safely avoid blur through camera movement. It will also overcome any blurring of slower moving subjects, particularly if some distance away.

If you want to 'freeze' moving subjects you will need a camera offering fast shutter speeds. The high jump athlete, Figure 4.2, was photographed at 1/250 second. Cycle races and autocar events will probably need 1/1000 or 1/2000 second to lose all blur, but much depends on the *direction* of movement and how *big* the moving subject appears in your picture as well as its actual speed. Someone running across your picture from left to right will record more blurred than the same runner moving directly towards you. If you are filling up your picture with just part of the figure – by shooting close or using a telephoto lens – movement is again exaggerated and needs a shorter shutter speed.

If you have a manually set camera

4.1

4.2 High jump (Courtesy Fowey School)

select a fast shutter setting, then alter the lens aperture until the meter reads correct exposure. On a semi-automatic or multi-mode camera choose 'shutter priority' (also known as 'Tv'), pick a fast shutter speed and the camera will do the aperture setting for you. When using briefest shutter speeds like this, it is helpful to shoot on fast film or work in bright light, or use a wide aperture lens – otherwise you may be under-exposing. If you have a simple camera with a fixed shutter speed try instead to swing ('pan') the camera in the same direction as the moving subject (see page 83). This can give you a reasonably sharp picture of your subject against a blurred *background*. See also flash, page 38.

Slow shutter speeds, say 1/30 second down to several whole seconds, may be necessary just to get a correctly exposed result in dim light like Figure 4.1, espe-

4.3 Ways of steadying the camera include tucking your elbows well in (centre) and using forehead or knee for extra support (right)

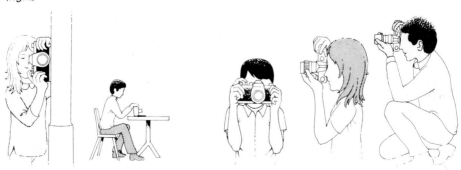

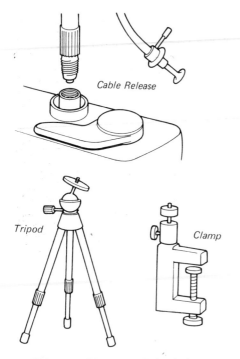

Cable Release

Tripod

Clamp

4.4 Aids to avoid camera shake during long exposures. Top: cable release, with lock. Bottom left: tripod. Bottom right: clamp for door or chairback

cially if you have loaded slow film or want to use a small lens aperture for depth of field. These longer times also allow you to show moving objects with different degrees of blur. Results often suggest action more strongly than having everything recorded in frozen detail.

Unlike using fast shutter speeds, however, you must take extra care to steady the camera, or camera shake will blur everything in your picture instead of just blurring moving elements. Figure 4.3 suggests ways of improving steadiness when using your camera hand-held. Learn to squeeze the shutter release button gently – don't jab it. Even then, if you use settings longer than 1/30 second, find a table, doorway or post and press the camera firmly against this. Your camera may display a 'shake' warning when it automatically selects a slow shutter speed. Be particularly careful when using

a telephoto lens because the larger image it gives magnifies camera movement, like looking through binoculars. By attaching a small mirror firmly to some flat part of the camera and then reflecting a torch off it in a darkened room (Figure 4.5) you can test how steady you are. If you can afford a tripod, or even a clamp which will secure your camera to the back of a chair, etc., this will allow steady exposures of unlimited length. Make sure though it has a pivoting head so you can angle the camera freely before locking it in place.

The range of slow shutter speeds offered on basic, manually set SLR cameras only goes down to about one second. If you want exposures longer than this you set the shutter to 'B'. The shutter then stays open for as long as the release button remains pressed, and you time your exposure with a watch. In practice it is best to use a screw-in cable release (or electric cable switch, advanced cameras) to avoid any risk of camera shake. Most of these releases have a lock, so you can leave the shutter locked open if necessary for really long exposures (Figure 8.14). Advanced, electronically-timed cameras allow you to set exposure times of 30 seconds or longer.

Long exposures times open up a whole range of blur effects that you can set up and control. As shown in Figure 4.6, for example, if you gave an exposure of several seconds you will get a different looking, increasingly abstract picture

4.5 Camera shake test

4.6 *Same exposure time, different amounts of bag swing. (Courtesy Sandra Campbell)*

according to how much you make your subject move. Pick something light and sparkling against a dark background, and use a small lens aperture so that you don't overexpose. (Some camera meters will not measure exposure for B settings, in which case 'cheat' the meter as described on page 83). There are great possibilities for interesting pictures using long exposure times when you try shooting moving lights at night. Use pages 82–6 as a guide.

4.7 *Panning with the moving players* $\frac{1}{60}$ *sec*

5 Aperture and point of focus

The smaller the size of your lens aperture the greater the range of objects at different distances you can show sharply focused in your picture. In both shots of the girl with apples, Figures 5.1 and 2, the lens was focused for the girl's hands. But whereas the top picture was taken at a wide aperture (an *f*-number of *f* 4) the bottom one was taken at a small aperture (*f* 16). The top result has a very shallow zone of sharpness (little 'depth of field'). Only where the lens was focused is really sharp – apples in the foreground and trees in the background are very fuzzy. The bottom result shows much more extensive sharpness (greater depth of field). Almost everything nearer and further away than the point of focus, the hands, now appears sharp.

Of the two versions the top one works best for this subject because it concentrates your attention on the two apple 'eyes'. The same applies to the horse's whiskers, opposite page. But on other occasions – the cornfield shown in Figure 5.4, for example – you may want to show all the pattern and detail clearly from just in front of the camera to the far horizon. So controlling depth of field in a picture by means of the lens aperture is a useful creative tool.

To get maximum depth of field first focus the lens for the key element in your picture or, if there is not one, for a distance about one third into the scene. In other words, if nearest important details are about 7 ft and furthest detail 25 ft from the camera, a difference of 18 ft, focus for about 13 ft. If you have a manually set camera select its smallest lens aperture (such as *f* 16 or *f* 22) then alter the shutter speed until the meter reads correct exposure. Using a semi-automatic or multi-mode camera choose 'aperture priority' (Av), set the smallest aperture your lens offers, and the camera does the rest. In poor light, unless you are using fast film, this may lead you to a slow shutter speed – so be prepared to use a tripod or some other means to steady the camera.

5.1–2 Changing aperture alters depth of field

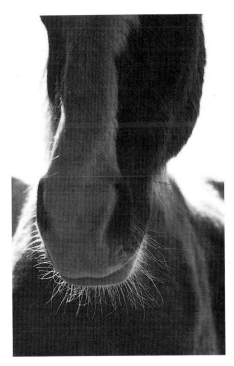

5.3 Shallow depth of field ('differential focus'). Aperture f2, normal lens

5.4 Deep depth of field, Aperture f 16, wide angle lens

SLR cameras are designed so that you always see the image on the focusing screen with the lens held open at widest aperture, which is convenient to view and focus. This is deceptive though if you have set a small aperture – just as you release the shutter the aperture changes to the size you set, so the picture comes out with far more depth of field than you saw on the screen. Some single lens reflex cameras have a depth of field preview button. Pressing this while you are look-ing through the viewfinder reduces the aperture size to whatever you have set, so you can visually check exactly which parts of a scene will be sharply recorded. (At the same time the smaller aperture makes the image on the screen become darker.) Another way of working, if you have time, is to use the depth of field scale shown on many SLR camera lenses, Figure 5.8. First, sharply focus the nearest important detail, in the example shown this reads as 3 metres on the focusing

5.5 F number scale

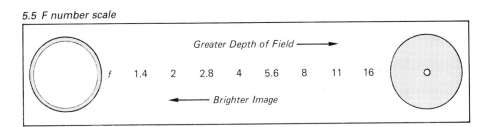

Greater Depth of Field ⟶

f   1.4   2   2.8   4   5.6   8   11   16   ○

⟵ Brighter Image

5.6 Wide aperture renders muddled background unsharp. Minimum depth of field concentrates attention on where the lens was focused (the boy's eyes and faces)

scale. Next, refocus for the furthest part you also want sharp, which might be 10 metres. Then, refer to the depth of field scale to see where to set focus between the two, and what *f*-number to use in order to embrace both 3 and 10 metres – in this case *f* 8.

On an automatic-only camera you will find that your pictures show greater depth of field the brighter the light and/or when fast film is loaded. This is because the camera then automatically sets a small aperture (along with brief shutter speed) to avoid overexposure. A typical fixed-focus compact camera is likely to have its lens set for about 4 metres with a fixed aperture of about *f* 8. In this way you get depth of field from about 2 metres to the far horizon, but remember that it remains unchangeable in every shot.

To get minimum depth of field. Carefully limiting your depth of field is a powerful way of emphasising the most important element in your picture and subduing unwanted detail at other distances – for example, the background in the shot of the boys above. You need a camera with a wide aperture lens and a really accurate method of focusing.

The standard, internationally agreed scale of *f*-numbers is shown in Figure 5.5. Each setting doubles, or halves, the brightness of the image; but the wider the aperture offered, the more expensive and bulky the lens becomes. A simple fixed-aperture camera may only offer *f* 8; most compacts have lenses which 'open up' to *f* 3.5 and 'stop down' to *f* 16. SLR standard lenses may offer a still longer part of the scale – from *f* 2 or *f* 1.4, to *f* 16 or *f* 22.

The wider the aperture you can set the less the depth of field possible. On a manual or aperture-priority mode camera using apertures such as $f2$ means that a fast shutter speed will probably have to be set, to avoid overexposure. In bright lighting it will be helpful to load slow film.

A further way of reducing depth of field is to use a longer focal length lens, or come closer to your subject. Changing to a telephoto lens (or setting your zoom to its longest focal length) gives less depth of field even though you keep to the same f-number.

Keeping depth of field to a minimum gives you very 'selective focus'. There is no margin for error in setting the lens for your chosen subject distance. Decide what the key element should be – in portraits it is usual to focus on the eyes; with sports events you might pick the cross bar of the high jump or just the sports track line a runner will use.

With an autofocusing camera it is vital to have the part of the scene you want sharp filling the tiny autofocus frame line in the centre of your viewfinder (see Figure 5.7). Then if necessary operate the camera's AF lock (often half pressure on the release) to maintain this focus setting while you finally compose the picture. Using the AF lock means you are not forced to have your selectively-focused

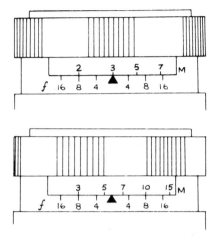

5.8 Depth of field indicator on lens. Top: When focused on 3 m depth of field at f8 is from 2 to nearly 6 metres. Bottom: focused on 5.5 m depth is 3–10 metres at f8

feature positioned centre frame every time. The degree of autofocusing accuracy your camera will give depends upon the number of 'steps' it moves through between nearest and furthest focusing positions. Fewer than 10 is relatively crude; to give the accuracy needed with a wide aperture lens at full aperture the system should have over 100 steps or be continuous. Most autofocusing SLR cameras allow you to change to manual focusing if you prefer to work this way.

5.7 Using the AF lock on an autofocus camera. 1: Centre your main subject in the autofocus rectangle. 2: Half depress the shutter release to make the lens focus, then press the AF lock on the camera body. 3: Re-compose your subject anywhere in the frame before taking the picture

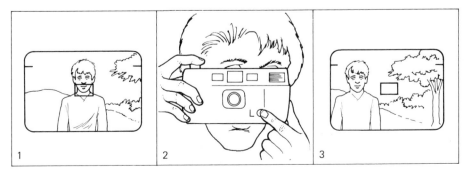

6 How much exposure to give

Essentially, giving 'correct' exposure means letting the image formed by the camera lens act sufficiently on your light-sensitive film to give a good quality picture after processing: neither too much nor too little. The negative shown below (top centre) has been correctly exposed. You can see from the print from this negative, shown directly beneath it, that plenty of detail has recorded in both the

6.1–6 (L to R) Under, correct and over-exposure of negatives, and the resulting prints

darkest shadows and the brightest parts of the picture. The same would apply to a colour negative film.

The negative on the left, however, has been seriously *underexposed*. Dark parts of the picture such as the boy's shadowed hands and his pullover have recorded as detail-free clear film – and appear feature-less black on the print below. Only the very lightest parts such as the puppy's white fur and the boy's hair could be said to show slightly more detail than the correctly exposed version. The negative on the right has been *overexposed*. So

much light has recorded in the highlight (lightest) parts of the subject they appear black and solid on the negative, white and 'burnt out' on the print. Only the pullover and hands show more detail than in the correctly exposed shot. (When you are shooting slides the same final differences apply, although there are no negatives involved.)

Choosing the settings. Most cameras make settings which will give correctly exposed results by: (1) sensing the ISO speed rating of the film you have loaded, (2) measuring the brightness of the subject you are photographing, (3) setting a suitable combination of shutter speed and aperture, either directly or by signalling when you have manually made the right settings. Simplest cameras having no exposure adjustments expect you to load an appropriately fast or slow film for your lighting conditions (page 17) then rely on the ability of modern films to give prints of fair quality even when slightly over- or underexposed.

If you are using a manual SLR you point the camera at your subject and alter either the shutter speed or lens aperture until a 'correct exposure' signal is shown in the viewfinder. This freedom of choice is like filling a bowl full of water either by using a fully open tap (aperture) for a short time (shutter) or a dribbling tap for a long time. The two pictures, right, for example, are both correctly exposed although one had 1/30 second at f 2.8 and the other 1 second at f 16. Each change to a higher f-number halves the light, so f 16 lets in only one thirtieth of the light let in by f 2.8, five settings up the scale. The pictures differ greatly though in other ways. The top one has very little depth of field but frozen hand movements; the other shows nearly all the keys in focus but the moving hands have blurred during the slow exposure.

A camera with automatic exposure (AE) automatically makes settings according to a built-in programme. This might start at 1/1000 second at f 16 for a very brightly lit scene then, if the light progressively dims changes to 1/500 sec-

6.7–8 A meter will tell you how the f-numbers and shutter speeds line up. You must then decide which to use. Here the top picture was given 1/30 second at f2.8, bottom picture 1 second at f 16. Both are correctly exposed but very different in appearance

6.9 Street with roughly even distribution of
light and dark tones. A general reading of
the whole scene here should give correct
exposure settings

ond at $f16$, and 1/500 second at $f11$, . . .
and so on, alternating shutter speed and
aperture changes. Such an automatic programme would never give results like
either Figures 6.7 or 6.8. It is more likely
to set 1/8 second at $f5.6$.

If your camera is fully automatic only
you will always get maximum depth of
field (combined with freezing of movement) in brightest light, especially if fast
film is loaded. This is why advanced AE
cameras also offer aperture priority
modes where you can set the f-number
and so determine depth of field, or use
shutter priority mode and set shutter
speed to control blur.

Advanced SLR cameras contain several automatic programmes designed to
make intelligent exposure setting decisions for you. When you change to a
telephoto lens the programme alters to
one using the aperture mostly to adjust
exposure, leaving the shutter working at
its faster speed to counteract the extra
camera shake risk from a long focal
length. If the camera offers a 'Sport and
action' mode this will give a similar
amme; whereas in 'Landscape'

mode the bias is the other way and the
programme aims to maintain as much
depth of field as possible.

Automatic exposure programmes are
very successful in giving correctly
exposed results from many different subjects and lighting conditions – see also
flash exposure, page 38 – but they make
their own assumptions about 'what set-

6.10 With two-thirds of this portrait black
background read exposure from close to
the face alone

tings are best'. So when you *want* blur in a sports picture or minimal depth of field in a landscape you must change to another mode, or switch to manual. A manually set camera in knowledgeable hands can still achieve the widest range of creative results from exposure.

Measuring different scenes. Most compact cameras have a small, separate window behind which a sensor responds to light reaching it from the whole of the scene you can see in the camera viewfinder. The so-called 'general' light reading it makes is accurate enough for subjects such as the street scene, Figure 6.9. You can see how the buildings that form a patchwork of light and dark range from dark-painted doorways in shadow to white stone walls in sunlight. But the areas taken up by really dark parts are roughly equal to the areas occupied by brightest parts, and all the rest of the scene is in medium tones approximately half way between the two. A general reading of the whole lot averages out all these differences, and the camera settings made will produce an exposure which is a good compromise for everything in the picture.

Simply averaging the whole subject area in this way will let you down occasionally though, if you want to shoot a picture such as Figure 6.10 or 6.11. The dog and wheelbarrow occupies less than half its whole picture area – the rest is much brighter sky. A general reading here would be greatly influenced by the sky, average out the scene as quite bright, and so make settings which underexpose the dog. The result might even be a black, featureless silhouette. The camera does not know that detail in dog and wheelbarrow is vital. Much the same thing can happen if you are shooting the interior of a building by existing light, and include a bright window. (See also fill-flash, page 41.)

In Figure 6.10 the opposite problem occurs. You need correct exposure for the man's face which is the vital part of this picture. But the largest area here is black

6.11 The big area of sky here makes a general reading underexpose

background, which would cause a general reading of the light to set exposure for a darker scene, making the face overexposed and 'burnt out'. Learn to recognize subject difficulties like this, but don't let them discourage you from shooting such pictures.

Different cameras help you overcome the problem in different ways. If your automatic camera has an exposure lock move closer until the face (or the wheelbarrow) fills up your entire picture. Then press the exposure lock so that the light reading made here is memorized and does not change when you move further back and compose the shot as you originally intended it. Using a manual SLR you should also come close, adjust aperture or shutter speed to get a 'correct exposure' signal, and keep to these settings when you move back again, even though over- or underexposure may then be shown.

Often SLR cameras use so-called 'centre-weighted' light measurement, meaning that they are designed to take more account of the broad central part of the picture – where the majority of main subjects are deemed to be placed. Advanced SLRs may offer a 'spot' read-

31

ing mode, whereby only a tiny area marked dead centre in the focusing screen is used to measure the light. You can position this over any key part, such as a face, even though you stay some distance away. A spot reading is very accurate and convenient, provided you understand what you are doing. In unskilled hands the spot area can easily stray to a completely wrong part of the scene. The result then is an exposure which produces a picture quite different to what you intended.

Do not become enslaved by the need for 'correct' exposure. Learn to recognise

6.13 A moody landscape helped by keeping tree detail underexposed and dark

6.12 A cast shadow shape

situations where carefully considering the way the light is read will vastly improve a shot. In Figure 6.13 for instance the tree is the main subject but it would be foolish to read exposure close up for the trunk. The result would then show detail of the bark but the amount of exposure needed would also give a featureless white sky. It is much more atmospheric to make the tree a shapely silhouette and preserve the background of grey misty cloud and a diffused sun. This was achieved simply by making an overall reading.

The brickwork girl, Figure 6.12, was a dark shadow cast onto a sunlit cream-painted wall by a figure just outside the picture. To measure exposure the camera was taken close to the shadow and settings made purely for this area. As a result brick details record only within this shape, leaving the rest of the wall burnt out. For yet another example look at the colourful deckchairs in Figure 9.4.

Pictures like these need sympathetic printing by your processing lab. Otherwise the lab could strain to 'correct' the very effect you wanted to produce. If necessary ask for a reprint, explaining what you were aiming for.

7 Changing lens focal length

The main effect of changing your lens focal length is that it alters image *size*, and therefore how much of your subject you 'get in'. A normal (or 'standard') lens for a 35 mm SLR camera is 50 mm focal length. On a 35 mm compact a lens of about 38 mm is most often fitted, mainly for space-saving reasons. These lenses give an angle of view of 46° or 58° respectively, see below, accepted as being similar to the field of view of the human eye.

Changing to a lens of longer focal length (also described as a *telephoto* lens) makes the image bigger. So you have a narrower angle of view and fill up your picture with only part of the scene. A change to a shorter focal length (a *wider angle* lens) has the opposite effects. But the more extreme these changes are from normal focal length the more unnatural the sizes and shapes of objects at different distances in your picture begin to appear.

Some lower-cost compact cameras come with a dual focal length lens – pressing a switch changes components inside the lens so it alters from, say, 28 mm to 45 mm. Other dual lens compacts might offer 35 mm and 70 mm. Most compacts have a zoom lens, changeable in steps or smoothly continuous. Focal length here might be 35–80 mm, or

7.1 Taken from the same camera position using (top) 135 mm telephoto, (centre) 50 mm standard lens, and (bottom) 28 mm wide angle

even 28–105 mm giving a four-to-one range of image size.

With an SLR you can just detach and interchange your normal lens for any of a range of wide angle or telephoto fixed focal length lenses. These could include anything from an extreme 8 mm fisheye

7.2 Different focal length lenses change angle of view. 50 mm gives about 46°, 28 mm lens gives wider angle

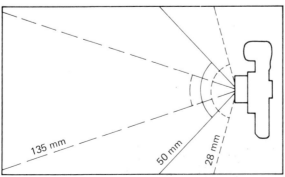

7.3 An 80 mm lens fills up the frame without coming too close

through to an extreme 1000 mm super telephoto. Alternatively buy your SLR with a continuous change zoom lens. This might be a middle range (28–70 mm) or a tele zoom (70–210 mm, for example) or wide angle range (24–50 mm). Bear in mind though that none of these lenses – zooms, wide-angles or telephotos – offer such a wide maximum aperture at such a reasonable price as a normal lens.

7.4 With a telephoto lens you can pick out inaccessible detail

Using a longer focal length. One reason for changing to a longer focal length lens is that you can keep your distance from the subject and yet still make it fill your picture. In portraiture changing to 80 or 100 mm allows you to take a head-and-shoulders shot without being so over-bearingly close that you make the person self-conscious, and create steepened perspective which distorts the face. Candid shots of children or animals are more easily shot from a distance with a 135 mm or 150 mm lens where you can keep out of their way. At sports events you are seldom permitted to approach close enough to capture action details with a normal lens. Both here and when photographing animals or birds in the wild a lens of 210 mm or longer is useful.

Long lenses are also useful for picking out high up, inaccessible details in architecture, and to shoot landscape from a distance so that mountains on the horizon look relatively large and more dominant. Remember, however, that you must be more exact with your focusing and take greater care to avoid camera shake than when using the normal focal length.

Using a shorter focal length. Changing to a wider angle lens such as 28 mm focal length is especially useful when you are photographing the interior of a room or building but cannot move back far enough with a normal lens to get it all in. It will also allow you to include sweeping foregrounds in shots of architecture or landscape (see Figure 15.2). The differences in scale between things close to you and furthest away are dramatically exaggerated. People seem more grotesque, even menacing. But focal lengths of 21 mm or shorter begin to distort shapes, particularly near the corners of your picture.

Controlling perspective. People say that the camera cannot lie, but with different focal length lenses you have almost as much freedom to control perspective in a

7.6 *Rooms tell you about people – a wide angle lens gets it all in*

7.5 *The startling effect given by an 8 mm extreme fisheye lens*

7.7 Whether you are drawing or photographing, a close viewpoint gives steepest perspective and size change. Moving back reduces the ratio of distances between nearest and furthest parts of the subject

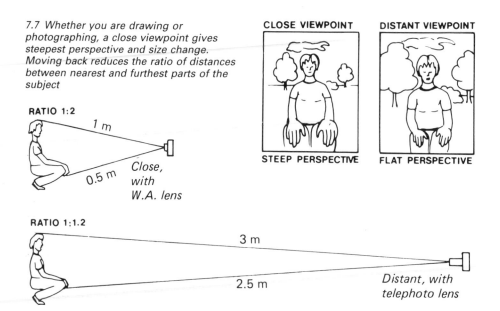

RATIO 1:2

1 m

0.5 m

Close, with W.A. lens

RATIO 1:1.2

3 m

2.5 m

Distant, with telephoto lens

CLOSE VIEWPOINT

DISTANT VIEWPOINT

STEEP PERSPECTIVE

FLAT PERSPECTIVE

7.8 Steep perspective. Photographed from a close viewpoint, using a wide angle (28 mm) lens

photograph as an artist has drawing by hand. Perspective is an important way of showing depth, as well as height and width in a picture. Elements appear smaller and closer together towards the far distance, and parallel lines seen obliquely seem to taper towards the background. The more steeply such lines converge (the greater the difference in scale), the deeper a picture seems to the eye.

As Figure 7.7 shows, it's all a matter of relative distances. Suppose you photograph (or just look) at someone from a close viewpoint so that the hands are only half as far from you as the face. Instead of hands and face being about equal in size, normal human proportions, the hands look *twice* as big. Perspective is steep. But if you move much further back, your distance from both hands and face become more equal. Hands are only *1.2 times* as big as the face. Perspective is flattened. Being further away too, everything is much smaller – but by changing to a longer focal length lens you can fill up your picture again.

So to create steep perspective the rule is to move close and then get everything in with a wide angle lens. A shot like Figure 7.8 makes you feel close to foreground objects and distant from the background. The man asleep is made important by his exaggerated scale. For flattened perspective move further away and change to a telephoto. In Figure 7.9, which was shot from a long way back with a 135 mm lens, there is little scale difference between the people nearest and furthest away. Compressed perspective gives a boxed-in feeling to the crowd.

Specialised optics. Extremely short or long focal length lenses give results so unlike human vision they are really special effects devices. Figure 7.5, shot with an 8 mm fisheye on an SLR, demonstrates its extreme depth of field as well as distortion (the building behind was one long straight wall).

Finally, if you have a continuous movement zoom lens, remember that changing focal length to enlarge up or reduce down image size whilst the shutter is *open* gives you a picture with streaks radiating from the centre. The picture below was given ¼ second at $f22$ on very slow film, zooming throughout exposure.

7.9 Flattened perspective. Distant viewpoint, long focus (135 mm) lens.

7.10 The effect of changing focal length on a zoom lens during exposure at a slow shutter speed

8 Using flash

Flash is a very convenient way of providing enough light for photography. After all, you carry it around built into the camera, its pulse of light is brief enough to prevent camera shake and freeze most subject movement, and it matches the colour of daylight. Unless you are careful though, flash gives harsh illumination slammed 'flat-on' to your subject, resulting in ugly and very unnatural looking lighting effects. Flash is handy when existing light is excessively contrasty or from the wrong direction, or impossibly dim for moving subjects. But don't allow flash to become the answer for all your indoor photography – especially if you can work using a camera with wide aperture lens and loaded with fast film.

Compact cameras can be used with flash at any shutter speed setting. SLR cameras, however, have focal plane shutters which at their fastest settings – typically beyond 1/125 second or

8.1 Flash built into (rear) SLR, and (front) compact cameras

8.2 Apertures for correct exposure at different distances with simple flashgun having a guide number of 12 (metres)

1/250 second according to design – only expose *part* of the frame at any one time (Figure 8.6). Avoid faster speeds because part of the picture will be missing. Advanced SLRs automatically avoid programming these unsuitable settings as soon as you select flash mode. On a manual SLR the fastest usable speed for flash often appears in a different colour, or marked with an 'X'. Remember that you can always use a *slower* speed safely, including 'B' setting.

Flash on the camera. A small flash unit is built into the body of most compact cameras, and some SLRs. Single lens reflexes also have a wired flash shoe ('hot shoe') to accept a more powerful slip-on flashgun. In all instances the flash fires triggered by the full opening of the shutter.

On a simple compact camera with no adjustments the flash gives sufficient light for correct exposure at the fixed aperture (typically *f* 5.6 using 100 ISO film) at one set distance (typically 7 ft or 2.1 m). A flash of this power is said to have a 'Guide Number' of 12 (5.6 × 2.1) (see page 152). Anything in your picture much closer or further away is either overexposed or underexposed. Most flash units, however, have a small light sensor pointing at your subject. The closer, or lighter your main subject the briefer the duration of the flash. The unit also picks up information about what film and lens aperture are being used (automatically through the camera circuit, or set manually) so your flash becomes self-regulating over a range of distances. Often these are 1.5–3.5 m.

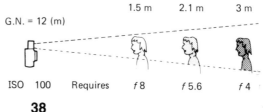

8.3 The worst effects of harsh flash, direct from camera

8.4 Flashgun further from lens and diffused with tracing paper

Unfortunately lighting your picture wholly with direct flash from beside the lens can create a number of unwanted effects. Several appear in Figure 8.3 above. A hard black shadow is cast onto the background one side of foreground figures. The pupils of the eyes appear red because the frontal light reaches the pink retina normally too dark to see behind the eye. Reflective surfaces square-on in the background glare light back towards the camera. One way to minimise these defects is to have your subjects close to any background surface to shorten shadows, the surface angled slightly to deflect reflections. 'Red eye' is reduced the further your flash is positioned away from the lens (Figure 8.4). Some flash units give a pulse of light just before they fire fully to take the picture, designed to make the eyes of the person you are photographing react by reducing their pupil size. Best of all work with an add-on flash unit indoors so you can tilt or swivel it to 'bounce' light off a white ceiling or wall onto your subject. This also gives a more even and natural appearance to your flash lighting (Figure 8.13).

39

8.5 Add-on flashguns. A, B & C; low and mediumpower units slip into the 'hot shoe' of the camera or connect by cable. C has tilting and swivelling head. Exposure measuring sensor (circular window) in each unit remains directed at subject. D: higher power flashgun with separate pack

8.6 Shutter blinds in many SLR cameras only uncover the full film frame at one time – here at 1/60 sec or slower speeds. At 1/125 or 1/250 flash only records part of the picture

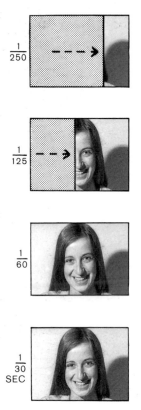

Another excellent way of using flash on the camera is as auxiliary or 'fill-in' illumination for the existing lighting present. When you shoot towards the light, as in Figure 8.9, a low-powered flash close to the lens illuminates what would otherwise be dark shadows, without looking false. An auto-focus compact or SLR camera which offers 'fill-flash' mode will make the necessary settings for you (selecting the aperture needed for flash at the distance you have autofocused, and the shutter speed for naturally lit surroundings at this aperture).

Fill-in flash from the camera is also useful for room interiors which may include a window and where the existing light alone leaves heavy black shadows (Figure 8.7). With different parts of the room at various distances from you, however, a direct flash may over-fill the foreground, yet under-fill furthest details. For still better results use a flash gun which allows you to bounce its light off a suitable wall or surface not included in the picture, producing a more even fill-in effect.

Bear in mind that there are limits to what you can fill-in (or light direct) with the flash power you have available. Don't expect to light a cathedral interior with amateur flash equipment. Using an auto-flash camera in the audience at a pop concert will probably just record people a few yards ahead, all the others disappearing into a sea of black. Avoid cameras which always switch on flash in dim light and so give you no options over results. *Using flash off the camera*. Flash does not always have to be positioned on the camera. You can have your separate flash gun connected via a long synchronisation cable which plugs into a camera socket or hot shoe (see Figure 8.5). The camera shutter still fires your flash, and exposure is still measured and controlled either by a sensor in the flash unit or the camera body.

Flash on extension gives you about the same freedom as using a separate lamp.

8.7–8 Controlling contrast. Right, daylight alone gives uneven lighting, ¼ sec f 16. Bottom, flash (at double power) bounced off wall, right, gently fills-in without giving shadows

Using the camera on one hand you can hold the flash out at arm's length, left or right. Or, you can set the flash up in just the right position attached to a chairback or tripod. This can be a good way to enliven close-ups of flowers and plants growing in shade, or photographed on an overcast day (see page 72).

Just remember that harsh direct flash from one side is like direct sunlight – fine for showing form and modelling but very contrasty. Where you don't want harshness set up a newspaper or white card as a reflector on the shadowed side of your subject, just out of the picture area.

Oblique flash lighting from one side will help to exaggerate the appearance of texture across a surface of stone or wood, as in Figure 8.11. Don't try to light too big an area, and keep the flash as distant as possible from the part you are photographing; otherwise your lighting will look uneven and unlike natural sunlight.

Another way of using a separate flashgun, without needing any extra equipment, is to use *open flash* technique. This means working in a blacked-out room, or

8.9 Flash on camera, set to 'fill flash' just lightens shadows

8.10 Overcast daylight alone

8.11 Raking light from flashgun held at arm's length gives sunlight effect

8.12 The natural-looking lighting effect
from an on-camera flash unit tilted
vertically to bounce from (off-white) ceiling.
The camera was set to fill-flash

8.13 Sole light source was on-camera flash
bounced off the ceiling. Pale toned
bathrooms are ideal for this technique,
provided ceilings are not coloured.
Compare with fig 8.3

outdoors at night. You set the camera up on a firm support and lock the shutter open on 'B'. Then holding the flash unit freely detached from the camera but pointed at your subject you press its flash test firing button. Having fired the flash once and allowed it to recharge you can fire it several more times each from different positions around the subject. The result looks as though you have used several lights from different directions.

Open flash allows you to photograph the garden or part of your house as if it was floodlit (see Figure 8.14). Calculate exposure from the guide number given for your flash. This is distance times the lens f-number needed. If the guide number is 30 (m) with the film you are using then set the lens to f8 and fire each flash from about 3.75 m (12 ft) away from its part of the subject. Plan out roughly where you should be for every flash, lighting a different area but without allowing the camera direct sight of either you or the flash unit. The total time the shutter remains open is not important provided there is little or no other lighting present.

Using open flash you can also create *stroboscopic* 'action' pictures of a moving figure. This time you keep the flash in one position, to one side of the subject. After each flash the figure changes position of an arm or leg, or the whole body. The result shows multi-limbs or a sequence of cloned figures.

8.14 'Open flash' shot of house at night using a basic SLR camera and separate flashgun. Camera, on tripod, had shutter held open by locked cable release. Photographer walked around firing flash about 20 times from widely different positions, each hidden from direct view of camera

PART THREE – ELEMENTS OF PICTURE MAKING

9 Seeing and photographing

Photographic films, cameras and enlargers are really no more than machines for making pictures. They cannot see or think for themselves. Of course it's quite enjoyable playing around with the machinery, and only taking pictures to test it out: but this is like polishing up your bicycle and only ever riding it around the block to see how well it goes. Bicycles enable you to get out and explore the world; just as cameras challenge you to portray things around you in new and interesting ways.

Anyone who wants to become a good photographer has to learn how to *see*. This means tuning yourself in to all the visual elements – shapes, patterns, colours, people's expressions, situations, etc. – surrounding you. It also means learning how to put that mindless machine (the camera), in the right place at the right time, to make the most effective image out of any of these subjects. Seeing and organising are just as important as technical know-how, and they come with practice.

To begin with it is helpful to consider how *seeing* differs from *photographing*. If you can forecast how the scene out in

9.1–2 Same shot, different cropping

45

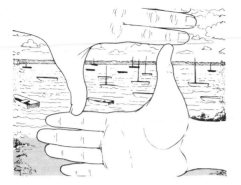

9.3 *Using your hands to frame up a scene*

focus and vague you are not really aware of any definite 'edge' to your vision. However, immediately you look through a camera the world is cut down into a small rectangle with sharply defined edges and corners. Instead of freely scanning your surroundings you have to compose their essence within this artificial boundary.

The hard edges and their height-to-width proportions have a strong effect on a photograph. Look how the same scene in Figures 9.1 and 9.2 is changed by format. Long, low pictures emphasise horizontal lines and space left-to-right; vertical rectangles emphasise height. You will find too that moving subjects can appear to be entering or leaving a scene depending upon whether they face close towards or away from one side of the frame. Even experienced workers often make a 'frame' shape with their hands to exclude surroundings when looking and deciding how a scene will photograph. And remember – nothing you leave

front of the camera will appear on your final print you can begin to use these differences creatively.

1. Pictures have edges. Our eyes look out on the world without being conscious of any 'frame' hemming in what we see. Stop a moment and check – your nose, eyebrows, glasses (if you wear them) do form a sort of frame, but this is so out of

9.4 *Where lighting picks out the interest*

9.5 Filling up the frame

outside the viewfinder can be added later!

2. The camera does not select. When we look at something we have an extraordinary ability to concentrate on the main item of interest. Our natural 'homing device' includes turning the head, focusing the eyes and generally disregarding any part of the scene considered unimportant. Talking to your friend outside his house you hardly register details of the building behind him, but the camera has no brain to tell it what is important and unimportant. It cannot discriminate and usually records too much – the unwanted detail along with the wanted. Drainpipes and brickwork in the background may appear just as strongly as your friend's face . . . and how did that dustbin appear in the foreground?

You therefore have to help the camera along, perhaps by changing your viewpoint or filling up the frame (if your camera will focus close enough) or use techniques such as less depth of field as discussed on page 26. Or, you could use the fact that the background has much less or more lighting than your main subject and then expose correctly for the latter only, as in Figure 9.4. Above all, take a quick look at *everything* you find in that viewfinder before pressing the button.

3. Film cannot cope with the same contrast as the eye. We can make out details in dark shadows and brightly lit parts of a scene (provided they are not right next to each other) which are well beyond the capabilities of a photograph. Photography generally makes darkest areas darker and lightest areas lighter than they appeared to the eye. To preview how your subject will photograph half-close your eyes and look through your eyelashes. Shadows now look much darker and the whole image more *contrasty*. This limitation of photographic film can be

9.6 For a moment in time figures here relate to one another forming an odd, surreal picture

camera's two-dimensional way of seeing by looking at the scene with one eye closed.

5. *Most photographs capture just one moment in time*. When things are active in front of the camera your choice of when to take the picture often 'sets' someone's momentary expression or the brief juxtaposition of one person to another or their surroundings, as in Figure 9.6. There is often a decisive moment for pressing the button which best sums up a situation or simply gives a good design. You need to be alert and able to make quick decisions if you are going for this type of picture. Once again the camera cannot think for you.

6. *Colour translated into monochrome*. When you are using black and white film the multicoloured world becomes simplified into tones of grey, black and white. A scarlet racing-car against green bushes becomes grey against grey. Try not to shoot pictures which rely a great deal on contrast of colours, unless this will also reproduce as contrasty *tones*. Look at colours as 'darks' and 'lights'. Remember too that an unimportant part of your subject which is much too strong and assertive (such as an orange-painted door in a street scene) can probably be ignored because it will merge with its surroundings on the final black and white print.

Occasionally you may need to alter the normal translation of colours into black and white and this can be done by using a coloured filter over the camera lens, see page 91.

used effectively, as on page 32 for example, but if you *want* full detail throughout your picture you may have to alter or wait for changes in lighting which reduce the contrast.

4. *The camera has one 'eye'*. Unlike humans, the cameras we are using do not have binocular vision. Their pictures are not three-dimensional. When we want to show depth in a scene we therefore have to *imply it* by use of converging lines, changes in scale, or changes in tones (Figure 14.2) aided by lighting. Remember you can always approximate the

PROJECTS

The projects appearing from time to time in the rest of this book are designed to improve your photographic seeing and awareness of picture possibilities and, of course, increase your technical ability. They are really a series of themes which can be tackled in any order, but progressively call for more things to consider. You will probably be able to find subjects in your locality for each project, even though they differ from the suggestions and examples shown. Don't try to copy exactly what is in the book. Approach each project as a chance to make discoveries.

Be on the look out for new ideas from every print – often you produce unexpected images which are worth following up to achieve something really successful. It's important to be adventurous, to break technical rules if results look interesting, but without losing control.

P9.1 Using clippings from magazines make a collection of photographs which all have a strong feeling of 'depth'. Sort these into groups such as (1) mostly achieved by use of line or scale; (2) by use of tone values; (3) by control of sharpness. Make up a scrapbook or display.

P9.2 Most cameras are used at eye level, so most photographs show the world from this height. Take six pictures of familiar subjects using your camera only *below* waist height or *above* normal head height. Display and discuss results.

P9.3 Using the home-made viewing tube or an adjustable sight on a ruler (Figure 9.7, right) practise framing up scenes. Make the distance between your eye and the 24×36 mm mask match the focal length of your camera lens. A cardboard slide mount is ideal.

9.7 With a home-made viewing tube or an adjustable sight on a ruler you can discover the effects of different focal length lenses

P9.4 Making appropriate use of colour, lighting, composition and expression take two portraits of the same person. One should show your subject as gentle and friendly, the other as sinister and frightening. Keep clothing and setting the same in each picture.

P9.5 Make a series of four photographs to illustrate one of the following relationships: (a) people and animals; (b) people and machines; (c) adults and children.

10.1 *The main element in this landscape, although small, is placed in a strong, dominant position*

10.2 *Picked out by colour and tone the lone bather appears to be about to perform some great feat, watched by figures on the distant promenade*

10 Creating emphasis

Most photographs are strengthened and simplified by having one main subject or 'centre of interest'. In a picture of a crowd, for example, this might be one figure waving a flag; a landscape might feature a cottage or a group of trees. Having picked this main element you can bring it into prominence and at the same time improve the structure of your shot by various means. The subject can be shown in a strong position relative to its surroundings because it appears to break the horizon or is placed where lines within your picture converge. It may stand out because of its contrasting colour or tone, or perhaps by the way it is framed within some strong shape either in front or behind.

Using lines. Lines are formed in a picture wherever lengthy, distinct boundaries

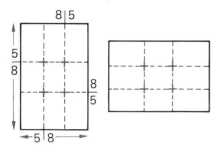

10.3 Intersection of lines gives 'Golden Mean' positions

occur between tones or colours. A line need not be the actual outline of an object but a whole chain of shapes – clouds, roads and hedges, shadows, movement, blur – which together form a strong linear element through a picture. Line shape (curved, straight) and their general pattern (short and steeply angled, long and parallel, etc.) can strongly influence the mood of your shot too. Compare the lively, radiating lines and curves of Figure 10.4, or the discord of Figure 22.1 with the calming effect of horizontal lines in Figure 10.8.

You can most easily control the appearance of lines in your picture by camera viewpoint – high, low, near, far, square-on or oblique, watching the way that one object overlaps or lines up with another behind it. Then change focal length if

10.4 A group 'held together' by the shape of the tyre, which also frames man at rear

10.5 Choice of viewpoint and wide angle lens, makes lines here link foreground with background

10.6 Tone difference separates subject from surroundings (Photo Doris Thomas)

necessary to fill the frame with just the area you need. Remember that you can also change height-to-width picture shape by cutting or masking the final enlargement (see page 134).

Position within the picture. Most beginners position the main subject they want to emphasise centrally in the picture, but there is a classical guide to placing the principal element called the 'golden mean' which artists have favoured in composition over the centuries. The concept is that the most pleasing position is at one of the intersection lines dividing vertical and horizontal zones in a 8:5 ratio. Figure 10.3 shows the four 'strong' positions this gives. The golden mean is an interesting compositional guide in photography but must never be slavishly adopted. Figure 10.1 uses this classical sort of placing; Figure 9.5 which has a symmetrical composition instead still works for its (exuberant) theme.

Forming 'frames'. One of the best ways to emphasise something, even when it is relatively small in your picture, is to show it surrounded by some naturally occurring 'frame'. The frame may simply be foreground foliage, or some building feature behind a figure. You can literally frame the portrait of someone by showing them reflected in a mirror on the wall (incidentally a good way to bring near and distant things together in the same picture). Frames can be made up from a mixture of cloud and foliage in landscape, like the subtle triangle shape around the building in Figure 10.1, or a clear-cut shape like the tyre in Figure 10.4. Cast shadows too can form frames of a sort.

Often unusual viewpoints give interesting framing – lower the camera to near ground level and use out-of-focus grasses (even milk bottles or a hole in a fence, if relevant) to fill the space. Foreground objects like this will not only emphasise a small distinct subject and give depth to a

10.7 Pedestrian underpass

10.8 Lead-ins and silhouettes

shot, but can obliterate large areas of irrelevant or distracting picture content you cannot avoid any other way.

Contrasting tone or colour. Making your main element the lightest or darkest tone, or the only item in a particular colour in the picture will pick it out strongly. This is also a good way to emphasise an interesting shape and help set mood (see page 58). If possible arrange that your chosen item is seen against the most opposite background. The eye is most attracted to where strong darks and light are adjacent, so make sure the emphasis really is where you want it to be. The Alice-in-Wonderland cat here and the figures in the tunnel both use this device – known as *tonal interchange*. Be careful to measure exposure to give the result you need (see Chapter 6).

With colour, greatest contrast occurs between a colour and its complementary (Figure 10.10) particularly when you make the area of one much smaller than the other. Certain hues also tend to be seen as 'coming forward' (red for example) whilst others such as blues or greens 'stand back'.

Once again you can often help to exploit contrast by your choice of background and viewpoint. For example, doorways are particularly useful – a figure outside a house can be isolated by careful alignment with a dark open entrance, or a coloured closed door. Don't allow the importance of your main subject to be diminished or camouflaged though, by overwhelming pattern or colour around it.

Of course, if you are photographing someone you know, or a largely 'still life' subject or landscape you usually have time to exploit this means of emphasis. But in a fast-changing, active situation often the best you can do is pick the most useful viewpoint and wait for the right moment. If foreground or background still prove confusing and irrelevant, de-clutter the picture by aiming high or low so that most of the frame is filled up with sky or ground. Alternatively use shallow depth of field or, if the subject is moving, pan the camera (page 83) at a shutter speed that will blur the unwanted detail. You can also choose a telephoto lens or use a closer viewpoint to cram the picture with your main subject, excluding everything else.

PROJECTS

P10.1 Find yourself a static subject in a landscape – an interesting building, a statue, even a telephone box or tree

10.9 *Emphasis through colour contrast*

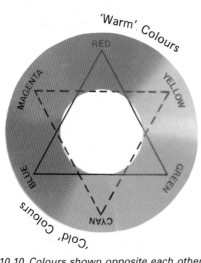

'Warm' Colours

RED
MAGENTA
YELLOW
BLUE
GREEN
CYAN
'Cold' Colours

10.10 *Colours shown opposite each other on this wheel are said to be 'complementary'*

– and see in how many ways you can vary your viewpoint and still make it the centre of interest. Utilise line, tone and colour.

P10.2 Make a series of three photographs of a figure in an identifiable environment – street, room, garden, etc. Your composition should use the figure (a) in the foreground; (b) in the background; (c) positioned near the corner of the frame, in each case balanced with or related to elements elsewhere in the picture.

P10.3 Produce three interesting pictures of objects or people in surroundings which can be made to provide strong lead-in lines, e.g. road and roof lines, steps, corridors, areas of sunshine and shadow. Make sure your subject is well placed to achieve maximum emphasis.

10.11 *Tight framing avoids clutter, simplifies lines and shapes*

11 Pattern and shape

Most photographs are 'subject orientated', meaning that who or what is featured in the shot is of greatest interest. Others are more 'structure orientated' – enjoyed not necessarily so much for subject as for the way the picture has been seen and constructed. In practice both aspects should ideally be present, if you want a unified picture rather than a random snap.

Pattern and shapes used in photographs are like notes and phrases used to structure music. They should be sought out and used as basic elements of composition. The fishing shot, right, uses different patterns at top and bottom (leaves, and water ripples) while interesting tree shapes help to enclose the figure. The picture is unified by its various tones of one colour, green. Figure 11.2 below relies on pattern alone, given life by variety of colours and shapes, like scattered pieces of a jigsaw puzzle.

11.1 A mixture of patterns harmonised by limited colour range – mainly green

11.2 Colours reflected from drops of oily water on new tarmac road surface

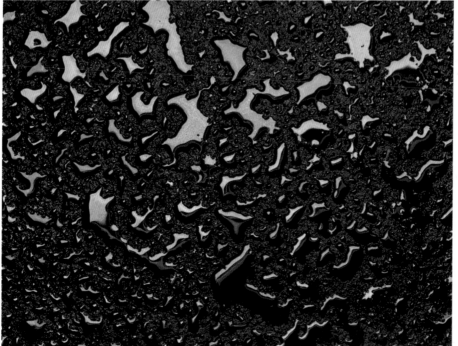

11.3 Shadow pattern

11.5 Related shapes

Shapes are often made stronger when repeated into a pattern, or echoed by a similar or contrasty shape somewhere else in the picture (see Figure 11.5). You can get a satisfying result from an almost (but not quite) symmetrical pattern, like Figure 11.8, or interplay between regular and irregular patterns, Figure 11.6. Sometimes too it's the *gaps between* objects, the bits of sky etc, which form a good shape or pattern of their own.

Patterns are frequently created by shadow. Harsh light can distort one pattern onto another, like the window bar shadows left. Much depends upon the lighting direction and height, and whether the surface receiving the shadow is flat or undulating, textured or plain. Shapes also gain strength from the way they contrast with their surroundings – the effect of background as well as lighting. The ultimate is a black and white silhouette like Figure 11.7.

The main problem with filling up your picture with pattern alone is that it usually lacks a core or point of emphasis. The result is like wallpaper. You can help matters by having one element in the pattern a completely different shape or colour. Or, create variety by having your shapes at various distances to give difference in size, perhaps shooting obliquely

11.4 Elephant hide

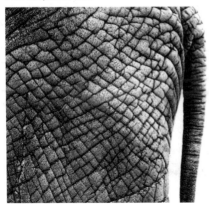

11.6 Contrasting but related patterns

56

with a wide-angle lens. Often appearance can be changed from a boring, meaningless shape to one which is interesting and significant, just by shifting position a few inches or waiting for the sun to move.

Look out for the possibilities of containing pattern wholly within a shape. This might be done by shooting through some appropriately shaped foreground object, or using a cast shadow combined with careful exposure control.

PROJECTS

P11.1 Using your camera as a notebook, analyse shapes found in your local architecture. Do not show buildings as they appear to the casual eye but select areas strong in design.

P11.2 Take four pictures which each include a *cast shadow*. Use your own shadow, or one cast by a variety of objects shown or unshown.

11.7 Objects silhouetted in front of a window or light box

11.8 Situations create patterns too

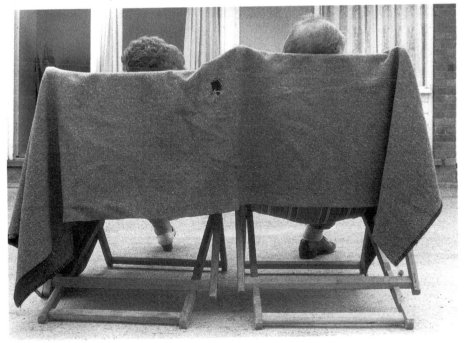

57

12.1 The warm colours of autumn landscape. Shooting from a distance with a telephoto helps to merge foreground and background leaves. Late afternoon sun.

12 Colour and mood

The so-called 'mood' of a photograph is influenced by its colour scheme, and its tonal values – proportions of light and dark. A picture full of brilliant, contrasting and intermingled colours has a lively, jazzy effect, but unless you are careful results will confuse and camouflage your main subject. One way to use intense colour effectively is to pack it all into a small enclosed area of your picture, contrasted by a larger more sober surround.

The brilliance of coloured subjects is greatly affected by lighting and weather conditions. When conditions are overcast a car which looks brilliant red in sunlight reflects light from the white sky in its polished surface and appears a diluted colour. Similarly, atmospheric haze or mist in a landscape scatters and mixes white light in with the coloured light reaching you from distant objects, so they appear less rich and saturated. Notice how colours in landscape are transformed and enriched when dull, overcast conditions change to direct sunlight after rain.

Colour has quite an emotional effect on pictures too. We associate certain colours or combinations of colours with other

12.2 A small splash of intense colour in the park during Spring

experiences. The comfortable feeling of a cottage interior or the atmosphere of an autumn landscape is intensified by warm colours. So decide carefully which coloured items you include or exclude from your shot.

A colour scheme making use of blues, greens, greys and similar 'cold' colours increases the bleakness of a winter scene, or an empty deserted house, or even inhuman appearance in a portrait. For extreme effects fit a coloured filter (page 91) or use the wrong coloured lighting for your film, such as the sodium street lights in Figure 12.3.

Black and white can be useful mood components in a colour picture. Black tends to make adjacent small areas of colour seem luminous and bright, like the oily water in Figure 11.2. Adjacent white helps to make colours look darker and stronger. The *overall* tone of the photograph is also important. A low key picture – one in which tones are mostly dark – can set a mood which is sombre, mysteri-

12.3 *Portrait illuminated by sodium street lighting*

ous or enclosed. A high key picture on the other hand can give a feeling of space, or light and happiness.

12.4 *The crispness of winter with its sparkling, back lit, frost. The cold blue colour scheme is mostly due to light from intense blue sky*

13 Texture

By revealing the texture in the surface or surfaces of your subject you help to make a two-dimensional photograph look three-dimensional. Texture also adds character to what might otherwise just be flat-looking slabs of tone and colour, helping to give your subject form and substance. All sorts of types and sizes of interesting textures exist around us. Weatherbeaten wood or stone comes immediately to mind, but look also at the texture of ploughed earth, plants, ageing peoples' faces, the (ephemeral) texture of wind-blown water, even rugged landscape where distant hills and mountains present texture on a giant scale.

There are two essentials for emphasising texture – appropriate lighting, and ability to resolve fine detail (accurate focusing and sufficient depth of field). Where the textured surface is all on one plane, like the wooden battens left, direct sunlight from one side separates out the raised and hollowed parts. The more the light skims the surface the greater the exaggeration of texture. If this means shooting partly towards the sun (Figure 13.2) take care to shade the lens with your hand or a hood.

Such extreme lighting also tends to leave empty black shadows – if these are large and unacceptable pick a time when white cloud is present in other parts of the sky, able to add some soft 'fill-in' light. (If you are working close-up you can often provide this yourself, holding up white or grey card to face your subject from near the camera).

When your subject contains several textured surfaces shown at different angles the use of harsh lighting from one direction may suit one surface but lights others flat-on or puts them totally in shadow. More diffused, hazy sunlight (but still directed from above or one side) will then give best results. What you can learn from sunlight can also be applied on a smaller scale, working with a lamp or flash off the camera, in the studio (see page 104).

PROJECTS

P13.1 Shoot three *transiently* textured surfaces. Suggestions: rippled water; clouds; billowing fabric; smoke. Remember the extra element here – choice of moment.

P13.2 Produce a series of close-up texture pictures. (Close-up technique, page 72). Explore a ball of string, a worn leather glove, or the sawn end of a length of wood.

13.1 Harsh, direct sunlight grazing the surface of weathered wood

13.2 Water texture

61

PART FOUR – TACKLING SUBJECTS

14 People

After looking at technical matters, and observation and picture-making in general, this part of the book is concerned with how different types of subject present their own photographic opportunities. The list of possible subjects is endless of course, but all of us sometime will want to photograph *people*.

People pictures might be of individuals or groups, posed or unposed. They range from subjects you know and can control, to candid shots of strangers. In all instances it pays to pre-plan your shot as far as you can – concern for background and setting, direction of the light, and how 'tight' to frame the person (full length; half length; head and shoulders; head shot). At the same time you must be able to respond fast to any fleeting expression or moment of action or reaction, as it may occur. For example, the mixture of uncertainty and achievement briefly shown by the little boy on the log opposite could be lost a moment later; similarly, the baby's raised head and open mouth in Figure 14.7.

14.1 Making an interesting shape

Babies are the least self-conscious people. The main problem is to manoeuvre or support a young baby so he/she is not just shown lying down. Try photo-

14.2 Give youngsters things to do

14.3 Hazy daylight avoids confusing shadows in this choir group. The pattern of faces and clothing (like musical notes) work best against a plain background

14.4 Boy's moment of balance – when anxiety turns into success

graphing over the shoulder of the supporting adult, or have the baby looking over the back of an armchair. Avoid direct, harsh sunlight, and if your camera offers a long focal length lens use this at its closest focus setting to get a large but undistorted image.

As children begin to grow up they quickly become conscious of the camera. It is often better then to 'give them something to do' – set up simple situations which are typical for the child, then wait for something to happen without over-directing the occasion. The girl looking through the letter box was a typical activity for the individual concerned, improvised on the spot for the photograph.

Remember the importance of lighting. Sunlight reflected from the far side of the white-painted door illuminated the child's eyes in Figure 14.2. When you are photographing a group of people however direct sunlight tends to give ugly shadows cast from one person onto the next. Softer, hazy daylight is best.

Groups should be organised into an overall shape without gaps. If they are dressed alike you can make use of pattern. The choir, above, creates a satisfactory pattern with every member similar in

14.5 Character portrait (Courtesy Roy Keith)

height and dress, and shown between simple bands of green hedge and black skirts.

With a posed portrait try to pick out some particular feature you want to stress. In Figure 14.1 the feature is the tattoos. A dark background combined with the man's dark trousers emphasises the shape

14.6 Figures placed to use foreground and background, but no mid-distance

of his arm, which also forms a lead-in to his face; working close with a slightly wide-angle (38 mm) lens increases the importance of the arm without noticeably distorting it. In all these instances the more you can *simplify* your picture the stronger and more *direct* it will be.

Portraying pairs of people allows you to relate them to each other in various ways. Figure 14.6 makes dynamic use of steep perspective and strong differences in scale, giving one figure a sense of dominance. This is another example of 'breaking the rule' to avoid using a wide-angle lens for portraiture. Fast film was necessary here, due to weak interior lighting and the need for a small aperture to get extensive depth of field.

Filling your picture with a single head avoids most problems of background and setting. Posed, characterful portraits such as the old lady above can be shot indoors

14.7 Babies are always unselfconscious

near a window, preferably on an overcast day for its soft, diffused light. Flash bounced off a wall on the right would give similar but visually less predictable results. It was taken with an 85 mm lens. Such one-sided lighting is excellent for texture and form, but sometimes vital details are lost into the shadows. For the baby shot, taken at floor level, a white towel was used on the left to reflect some daylight back into the shadow side of the face.

Candid shots of strangers are easier if you begin in crowded places like a market or station where most people are concentrating on doing other things. Observe situations carefully, especially relationships (real or apparent). These may occur between people and pets, or notices, or other people. Often you can discover a good background or setting, then wait for interesting passers-by to enter your shot (see Figure 9.6). But don't obstruct people when photographing in the street, and always ask permission to shoot on private property.

15 Places

Unlike people, 'places' (landscapes, buildings, etc.) are fixed in position relative to their surroundings. This does not mean however that picture possibilities are fixed too, and you cannot produce your own personal portrait of a place. It is just that good, interpretive shots of cityscapes or landscapes require more careful organisation of viewpoint, and patience over lighting, than most people imagine. The best picture is seldom the first quick snap.

Compare the two approaches to concrete architecture on this page, for example. The version below is a dynamic and

15.1 (Right) A viewpoint chosen to produce false attachment of foreground to background gives a caged-in feeling to this building

15.2 (Below) A picture making strong use of linear perspective and size change to convey depth. (28 mm lens)

generally optimistic shot of a space-age environment; the other shows the tower block as some sort of prison, cut off from the rest of the world. The first shot achieves its effect through a viewpoint giving steeply angled lines that sweep you into the picture. A wide-angle (28 mm) lens has included plenty of close foreground resulting in dramatic scale change between the nearest and most distant detail. Time of day was chosen when sunlight comes almost from the rear, increasing the depth effect.

For the tower block a distant viewpoint, flat-on to the wall was carefully selected by eye – to align wall, tower and shadow, and make them seem connected. The effect is one of shallow space, with wall and railings 'attached' to the tower and caging it in. The lens focal length was set to 80 mm to fill up the frame from this spot.

When you visit a famous town or city for the first time there is little point in trying to repeat tourist views you can buy easily as postcards. Instead try to give yourself time to soak up the atmosphere of the place, to form your own impressions. Then decide what to photograph as *your* memories of the visit. Sometimes the famous bits can just be suggested, through a reflection or shadow (see Figure 15.8). Or, you may want to bring together selected details with a set of pictures like the collection of front doors, Figure 15.6. You can often sum up a whole part of town by just showing part of one building (see Figures 15.3 and 15.7). Signs and logos form titles.

Think out the sun's movement and be prepared to come back at the time of day when its direction will best suit what you

15.3 (Above) Sometimes signs can be used as titles

15.4 Mid-afternoon

15.5 Mid-morning

need to show. Similarly choose between weather conditions that will give clear direct sunlight, or soft diffused light. The best times for interesting, changing lighting effects are either in the early morning or late afternoon. Don't overlook the transformation of building exteriors at dusk, when internal lighting brightens the windows but you can still separate building shape from sky.

Choosing time of day and weather are just as important for country landscapes. The two pictures above contain the same components but lighting has greatly altered the impression of colour and depth. Figure 15.5 was taken mid-morn-ing with sunlight from one side, slightly frontal. In Figure 15.4, several hours later, the sun is further to the rear. This change plus heat haze increases depth but reduces colour and detail. Aim to include some main feature – a hill shape or cottage perhaps, or as in this case just a moored boat.

Generally avoid splitting your pictures in the middle with the horizon. Place it above or below centre frame instead. Try to avoid empty foregrounds by finding a viewpoint which fills this area with foliage, or just shadow pattern. Remember the value of lines and shapes which might 'lead you in'.

15.6 A series on doors can be planned and presented as a row of prints which create your own complete made-up street

15.7 Wall painting, New York

PROJECTS

P15.1 Take two photographs of places to emphasise each of the following contrasts; ancient/modern; man-made/natural; formal/eccentric; cherished/neglected.

P15.2 Sum up your impressions of one of the following in 1–3 pictures. (a) a graveyard; (b) the seashore; (c) a modern industrial park.

15.8 In the shadow of the Eiffel Tower

16 Animals

Photographing family pets and rural animals is rather like photographing young children. You need a lot of patience because they cannot be told what to do; they are unselfconscious (although capable of showing off); and their relationships with people are a great source of situation pictures.

Always take the camera to the animal rather than the reverse. In other words, don't put the animal in a false or unfamiliar environment just because this is more convenient for your photography. Animals do not really belong in studios.

16.1 Size can be shown by the scale of this dog's surroundings

16.2 Scared kitten behind its front door

Instead decide what is a typical activity and environment for your particular pet. Maybe it is good at leaping for balls, rolling on its back, or just lapping up milk? Just setting up simple situations – a ball on a string or a throwable stick – may be enough to draw out the individual character of your animal. Don't over-manage and degrade your pet by, say, dressing it up or putting it into ridiculous situations.

Your viewpoint and distance can help to emphasise size – a looming great horse seen close from a low angle with a standard lens, or a minute pup in front of a mountain of crates and casks taken from across the street with a telephoto. A telephoto lens is also useful just to pick out the detail of a characteristic *part* of a large animal, such as the rhino, Figure 11.4. Make background and surroundings relevant to your animal, showing something of its favourite habitat (Figure 16.1). Alternatively, keep to a plain background such as sky or grass.

Having a helper is very useful to control the animal and if necessary attract its attention at the key moment. Another approach is to give the animal time to lose interest in you and your camera and return to its normal activities, like dozing in the sun. Have all your camera controls for exposure set in advance, or on automatic mode. Use fast film, fast shutter speeds, and watch your animal through the viewfinder all the time, to be ready to shoot the most fleeting situation. A rapidly autofocusing camera is particularly helpful when an animal is liable to move about unexpectedly, and is also close.

As with candid shots of people, the richest source of animal relationship pictures is at gatherings – pet shows, livestock markets, pony races, farm yards, even dogs' homes – where plenty is going on. Avoid using flash, especially at competitive events where animals might shy; also, 'red eye' from flash on the camera is just as prevalent with animals as human beings.

16.3 *Low angle gives strong, simple shapes*

PROJECTS

P16.1 Produce two or three interesting animal 'head and shoulders' portraits of either: (a) a dog; (b) a tame rabbit or hamster; (c) a cat. Try to convey *character* through showing what they most like to do. Include the owner if relevant.

P16.2 Find and photograph two types of farm or pet animals with their young.

P16.3 Make a short series of pictures of *owners* and *pets* to prove or disprove the theory that they grow to resemble one another.

17 Close-up subjects

Working close-up (within a foot or so of your subject) opens up a whole new spectrum of picture possibilities. You can not only record small objects so that they fill the frame, but strong, often dramatic pictures can be made from just details of larger, quite ordinary things. A cabbage, or a few clothes pegs . . . or just the page edges of a thick book are examples of hundreds of simple subjects that can be explored for hours in close-up. Along with plants and flowers, and weathered or corroded materials, they provide a rich source of pictures based on colour, shape, pattern and texture.

The main technical problem is how to get a really sharp image when working this close. You firstly have to overcome the fact that a camera lens must be located further forward of the film (or greatly shorten its focal length) to focus a close subject. The degree of change needed here accelerates rapidly the closer you come. (For Figure 17.4 with the subject 27 cm away the lens was 6.1 cm from the film for sharp focus, but when only 9 cm from the insect, Figure 17.5, a lens-film distance of 11.2 cm is necessary).

Secondly, depth of field is increasingly shallow, even at a small aperture. This means that your focusing must be very accurate – there is little latitude for error – and, unless your subject is all at one distance you may find it impossible to record detail in parts nearer or further away at the same time. A third point is that working this close magnifies image *movement*, so be prepared to support the camera firmly, or use flash as your light source to avoid blur.

17.1–2 Left: exposed for flash alone. Right: at quarter power flash just provides fill-in

17.3–5 Top: Normal lens at closest setting. Centre: with 1 cm ring added. Bottom: with 5 cm tube

17.6 It helps to use a viewpoint from which all your main subject is the same distance from the lens

Whilst a compact camera may have a so-called 'macro' focus setting this is rarely for subjects closer than 60 or 45 cm. The viewfinder is not accurate closer either. An SLR camera always gives you an accurate view, and since the lens can be removed you can usually attach one or more extension rings to space out your (normal focal length) lens from the camera body for close work. Bellows, Figure 17.7, serve a similar function but are continuously adjustable,

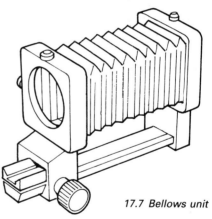

17.7 Bellows unit

17.8 Lit by daylight through tracing paper

17.9 F 16 chosen to get reflection and eye sharp

17.10 Situation still life

and longer. Autofocus lenses have to be manually focused. Most SLR zoom lenses offer a *macro setting* on the focusing scale. This adjusts components inside the lens so you can sharply focus subjects an inch or so from its front surface. Often the range of subject distances is very restricted. For best quality and greatest flexibility in close-up work change your SLR camera lens to a more expensive macro lens, specially designed for close subjects. Its focusing scale allows continuous focusing down to about 20 cm and thereafter closer still if you add rings or bellows.

Where possible have all the parts of your subject you need to show as pin-sharp about the same distance from the lens (see Figure 17.6). The easiest way to focus is to set subject distance *approximately* (or select lens closest distance setting) then look through the camera viewfinder and sway slowly towards and away from your subject until the image appears sharp. The very critical focusing needed for Figure 17.9 was done this way.

Fast film is clearly an asset if you are working at small aperture for depth of field and trying to keep to a shutter speed permitting hand-held use of the camera – especially with insects and wind-blown flowers on the move – but avoid extra fast, grainy films which may destroy finest detail. You can also make good use of flash – partly for its brief but powerful illumination close up, partly to control subject appearance. With fixed subjects like plants you can use flash on the camera to suppress surroundings, or just fill shadows leaving sunlight to pick out form (see Figure 17.2). Alternatively have the flash positioned away from the camera as your main light (see page 42).

Recording still lifes. Being able to work close up means that you can freely set up inanimate objects indoors – to photograph them either for record purposes, or as still life compositions. This is a good way to explore lighting (Chapter 25) and composition. A tripod will enable you to position the camera in one spot, then build up your picture bit by bit. Still lifes can be 'found objects' such as Figure 17.11, which is a kind of portrait of its owner. They might relate two items directly as in the picture above, or simply be put together as a mixture of contrasting or similar shapes and forms, like Figure 17.12.

17.11 Boy's pocket contents

PROJECTS

P17.1 Make a still life photograph on the theme *paper.* Include corrugated card, tissue, writing and wrapping paper. Fill up the frame.

P17.2 Photograph some of the materials and tools used for either: (a) dressmaking; (b) woodwork; (c) cookery.

P17.3 If you have some small valuable items record them for insurance purposes. Include a ruler alongside for scale.

17.12 Still life oddments

18 Working to a theme

A good way to extend your photography is to work to a particular topic or theme – something chosen yourself, or set perhaps in a competition. This challenges you to organise ideas and plan your approach, and actually having to carry out an assignment makes you solve technical problems, gaining experience and confidence.

Themes might place greatest emphasis on picture *content*, or mostly on *structure*, or underlying *concepts and ideas*. Results might be a single picture, or a pair or (most often) a sequence of photographs. One picture can sum up a simple concept such as joy or sorrow; it can also make strong comparisons if it divides naturally into two 'compartments' using a doorway, window or mirror. Two separate photographs offer greater freedom for comparisons and contrasts when presented together. Aim to keep some features (background, lighting, position in the frame) similar in both pictures to show up differences in your main subjects. A longer series of pictures gives scope to tell a story or explain a process, show changes of time and place, develop a theme.

Portrait themes. Think of all the ways you can show an individual – at work, at home with their possessions, with family and friends, travelling, relaxing or practising a hobby. You need patience and time to get to know your subject well, observing mannerisms, seeking out representative aspects of their life.

Another way of working is to shoot a 'collective portrait', one picture of every family in a street or apartment block. Here you might show each at their own front door, keeping your viewpoint and lighting similar to provide continuity. Allow the groups to pose themselves. Even show their reactions to being photographed – some showing off, others shy.

Themes based on structures. Here the main common element may be simply movement, colour, or shapes. Make a series from 'found' subjects which share a common colour scheme (see facing page) but have many variations in content, scale, etc. Aim to make each shot a satisfying image within itself too. To begin a project on the theme 'light', for example, you could consider qualities such as brilliance, reflection, colour, cast shadow and so on. Observe the effects of light on various surfaces under different atmospheric conditions. Next work through your list, eliminating similarities and identifying six or so characteristics you want to show. Then find suitable subjects (don't overlook the macro world) and techniques to communicate strongly each aspect.

Narrative/documentary themes. A story or narrative thread might illustrate a poem, or cover a passage of time or a journey from one place to another. Picture series need visual *variety* but also *continuity*. Start off with a strong general view as an establishing shot, then move in to concentrate on particular areas including close-ups and lively (but not puzzling) viewpoints. The final photograph might bring the viewer full circle, e.g. the opening picture re-shot at dusk.

For the broader documentary themes it is seldom possible to give in-depth coverage from a single visit. Get to know the subject, or area, so that you can develop an informed point of view. This way your pictures will have something to say.

PROJECTS

P18.1 Using hands as an expression of emotion, produce three pictures, each conveying one of the following – anger, tenderness, tension, prayer.

P18.2 Illustrate three of the following themes using a pair of pictures in each case: simple/complex, young/old, tall/short, hard/soft.

P18.3 Make a documentary series of four pictures on either 'Children at Play', or 'Shopping', or 'A Day Off'.

18.1–7 *A theme simply based on seeking out and using one dominant colour*

19 Assessing results from the lab

Everyone makes mistakes, sometime. But when you receive back unexpected results from processing it's important to identify what went wrong. Was it the film . . . or the camera . . . or (most likely) the way you used your equipment? Or maybe it's all due to the lab which processed and printed your results?

The most disastrous sort of results are shown below and opposite – where a whole film contains no pictures at all. Where you have prints to judge the first thing is to compare them very closely against the returned negatives (the film exposed in the camera). If a negative looks normal and shows a lot more detail than its print, or the print shows a blemish which cannot be seen on the negative, ask for a reprint. If you have shot slides it is often easier to pin down faults – the chain of processing does not then include printing, a stage where incompetence or attempts to salvage results can confuse the cause.

The prints and slides reproduced over-leaf form a cross-section of typical basic faults. Test yourself by guessing their cause, then check below against the appropriate alphabetic reference. Some others appear on page 128. Comments apply to colour prints or negatives, slide films only if stated.

No images at all

A Colour or monochrome negative film heavily fogged to light, or (negative or slide) chemical fogging during processing.

B Negative film vastly overexposed to light through the camera shutter. Perhaps the shutter was incorrectly on 'B', or the aperture failed to stop down.

C Negative film moved through the camera with the shutter jammed open. Probably occurred during rewinding.

D Since the film's data (factory printed by light) is also missing here the cause is

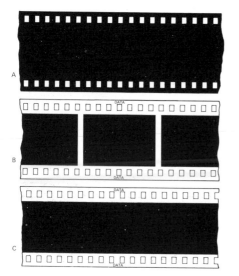

19.1

faulty processing. If *slide* film the cause is as for **A**.

E Unexposed negative film. An unused cassette sent for processing perhaps; or film jammed; shutter failed; or (SLR) mirror jammed down.

F Slide film unexposed. Causes as for **E**.

Pictures, but with faults

G The best possible print from severely underexposed negative. A simple camera with slow film used in dim lighting.

H Slide underexposed by at least two *f*-number or aperture settings.

I Overexposed slide, or a print from an overexposed negative. Film given four times correct exposure. Perhaps one-quarter correct ISO set; or (SLR) lens aperture jammed open?

J Underexposed. Metering system too influenced by bright light from window. Needed reading of foreground figures only, then AE locked; or fill-flash. Slide similar.

K Misfocus by AF system. Print or slide. Central focus-measuring zone coincided here with doors in background.

L 'Necklace' of flare spots caused by shooting towards sun. Shade lens with your hand or lens hood. Print or slide.

M Camera shake. Print or slide. Unlike subject movement even static elements are blurred. Needed a faster shutter speed. Alternatively flash.

N Viewfinder parallax error, compact camera. Print or slide.

O Flare from flash, reflected off top of incubator. Shoot from more of an angle or avoid flash on camera. Print or slide.

P Obstruction (finger tip) just in front of lens. Print or slide.

Q Bands of fog across the film, caused by partly opening the camera before rewinding. Print or slide.

R Unexpected lettering (on right) due to splice put onto very end of film by lab. Don't try squeezing on an extra picture. Print or slide films.

S Uneven flash. Print or slide. Probably caused by hand partly over flash unit.

T Front or end of film fogged at mouth of cassette. Perhaps not fully rewound when film removed from camera. Print or slide.

U Hair on film surface when shot taken. Check space between film and lens. Print or slide.

V Hair temporarily on negative surface during printing. Often easy to 'spot out' on print, see page 131. Alternatively request a reprint.

19.2

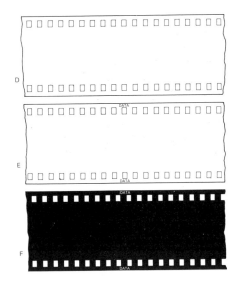

G   Flat, grey, lacking shadow detail

H   Shadows black, detail in light parts

I   Bleached looking, detail in shadows

J   Main subject too dark

k   Only background sharp (AF camera)

M   Everywhere streaked and blurred

L   Line of white spots and beads

N   Part missed off

80

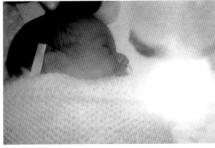

O   Glare off plastic window

P   Dark patch, bottom right

Q   Patches of orange and red

R   Ghost image of lettering

S   Lighting fades off, one side

T   Coloured band with distinct edge

U   Black hair shape

V   White hair shape

20 Movement and abstraction

Don't become too fixed in your ideas about what makes a technically good photograph. Successful pictures don't all have to be fully detailed and free of blur. Sometimes an 'error' gives you an image which sums up an event or expresses a subject better than the result you expected. You can then explore this approach further, in order to expand your picture-making skills. It's also great fun.

20.1 Fairground wheel, late dusk

Very few of the techniques in this section call for equipment beyond a camera offering a 'B' setting shutter. On the other hand they are all suggestions for experiments so you must be prepared to waste film on a trial-and-error basis. Even professionals expect to shoot many frames for one good result. Take a range of versions of your subject making notes of the settings used. Then if necessary make further experimental shots based on the best results.

The painter Paul Klee once said that 'a line is a dot that has gone for a walk'. In photography as soon as you allow the image to move while it is exposing every dot highlight gets drawn out into a line. We are all used to blur indicating movement, from close objects rushing past the car window, to the streaks drawn behind characters in comic strips. Something moving slowly can be made to appear to be travelling fast by giving it a long exposure time, or something fast appear slow or stationary by using a very brief exposure time. Similarly your subject can appear to have bumpy or smooth motion according to the shape of the lines, which you can control by jerking or gliding the camera.

Keeping the camera still. Long exposure times with the camera kept absolutely still (on a tripod for example) record static parts of a scene clearly but elongate bright moving parts into light trails. The double big wheel (Figure 20.1) was shot at late dusk giving 2 secs at *f* 8 on ISO 400 film. The top wheel was turning very slowly, about once in 25 seconds, but since it moved through about 30° during exposure it seems to be rotating fast. Shooting at dusk gives just enough light in the sky to separate out the dark superstructure.

Some AE cameras will measure and give this sort of exposure time, provided you can select aperture priority mode and set a small aperture. With manual SLR cameras the meter may not function for long exposures and will need 'cheating'. For the wheel shot, for example, setting the aperture to $f2$ makes the meter respond with ⅛ second, and from this you can calculate that at $f8$ you should give 2 seconds held open on 'B'.

The geometric patterns formed by moving points of light are sometimes quite unexpected because they are normally too slow for us to see. The starlit night sky, Figure 20.3, was exposed for 1½ hours at $f16$ on ISO 125 film. The camera was left pointing generally towards the pole star, around which other stars appear to move. Pick a clear moonless and wind-free night, well away from any pollution of the sky by street lights.

20.2 Panning technique

20.3 Star tracks at night

20.4 Girl's face, moving at same speed as the panned camera, records sharply at 1/60 sec

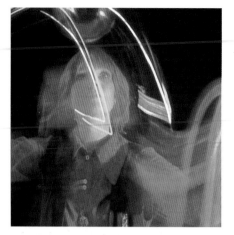

20.5 *A time exposure in the studio as the girl waved plastic sheeting. Daylight colour film, studio lamps*

Panning the camera. By hand-holding the camera and pivotting your body you can follow a fast moving subject by 'panning'. Swing the camera smoothly and release the shutter in the middle of the pan. All the most static elements then blur and only the main subject you followed steadily in the frame appears clearly. A shutter speed of ⅓₀ second is often about right (⅙₀ second for very fast movement

20.6 *Patterns formed by moving the camera around with its shutter open in a city street at night. Exposure 15 secs at f 16*

like Figure 20.4). Set AE cameras to shutter priority mode, at this setting.

Still plus moving. One way of enlivening totally static, lit subjects at night is to give part of a (long) exposure with the camera first still, and then moving. The still part of the exposure records the general shape of the subject and the moving part shifts all the highlights. In Figure 20.7, for example, the camera was loosely attached to a tripod. It was held firm for the first half of a 3 second exposure at ƒ22, and then panned left at 45° throughout the final 1½ seconds.

If you are working with people you can keep the camera firmly on a tripod throughout, and get your subject to remain very still when the shutter opens – until you cue them to move. The girl in Figure 20.5 was given a 4 second exposure, at ƒ16. After the first second or so she moved her arms rapidly, waving clear plastic sheeting which reflected (orangey) studio lamps. Try this sort of disco image in the garden at night, using domestic lamps.

Writing with light. As a further experiment, if you have a steady hand, it is possible to write or draw designs in light. Work outdoors at night, or in a darkened room with a black background. Secure the camera to a tripod and mark out on the ground the left and right hand limits of your picture area. Your 'performance' must not exceed these extremes. Focus on a newspaper, lit by hand torch, held midway between the markers. Set the shutter for 'B'.

To produce Figure 20.8 someone wearing dark clothes stood between the markers facing the camera. Keeping on the move they 'wrote' in the air with a lighted 'sparkler' firework whilst the shutter remained open. A small handbag type torch makes a good light pen too, provided you keep it pointed towards the camera as you write. Torches with built-in colour filters allow the lines to change colour, or you can organise someone to use a series of filters over the camera lens. Exposure varies according to the strength of light and speed of drawing. Test at

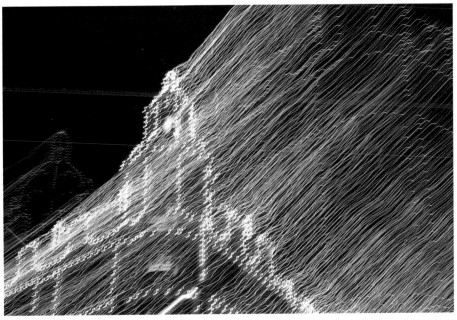

20.7 Not on fire, but produced by shifting
the camera part way through exposure

20.8 Below: Drawing with a sparkler in the
dark

about f16 for a total writing time of 10 seconds (ISO 100 film). Write at a consistent speed – slower lines thicken through overexposure, fast lines record thin. Words and numbers will appear wrong-reading to the camera so you should have the negative printed, or slide projected, through the *back* of the film.

Another way of creating 'drawn' light patterns is just to move the camera about with the shutter open at night. Pick an area with many distant traffic lights, street lights and illuminated signs of different colours. In Figure 20.6 the shutter remained open for 15 seconds at f16, with the camera constantly on the move.

Distorting reality. With experience you can move, or zoom, a camera with the shutter open so that the blur lines are sympathetic to the interpretation you need. In Figure 20.9 the camera was panned, inaccurately, for ⅛ second in a gentle curve. The car becomes softened and more streamlined. A jerky pan would have suited an old jalopy.

The wild looking wood in Figure 20.10 was created by making three exposures onto one frame of film. The camera was rotated a few degrees about a horizontal axis between each exposure. It is best to use a manual SLR for superimpositions like this – you keep the rewind button in the base pressed when winding on after each exposure so that the film remains in place. Some advanced cameras offer special superimposition mode.

Interpretive semi-abstractions can happen through 'straight' camera techniques too. All three pictures overleaf have had their subject shapes altered in simple optical ways. The swimmer is partly distorted through refraction by the water. Such a picture is easy using a telephoto lens from the side of a swimming pool. The two children were pressed up close behind patterned glass. To make these shapes work it was important to have a window lighting the wall behind their heads as well as another from the right on their faces. The shot of the tree with clouds shows more subtle changes. Everything is reflected in almost still water, and the picture is presented here upside down.

20.9 Gliding impression of speed on highway

20.10 The wild wood

PROJECTS

P20.1 Produce pictures showing: (a) slow subjects – elderly people, milk floats, tortoises, fat animals, etc., apparently whizzing along; (b) fast subjects made to appear stationary or moving very slowly.

P20.2 Mount the camera firmly on your bicycle handlebars. Shoot pictures at ⅛ second shutter speed or slower, whilst cycling through a busy part of town at dusk. (Don't look through the viewfinder – keep your eyes on the road!)

P20.3 Walk around a fairground or lighted traffic-filled streets at night, holding the camera with its shutter open for 3–5 seconds (at f16, ISO 125 film). Include plenty of pinpoint lights. Keep the camera still for part of each exposure.

P20.4 Make a series of abstract colour images of the human figure. Consider the possibilities of focus, movement blur, reflection, refraction, and shoot-ing through various semi-transparent materials.

20.11 Appearance distorted by refraction through water

P20.5 Create physiogram patterns. In a darkened room rest your camera on the floor pointing upwards, focused for one metre and set to $f8$ (ISO 100 film). Suspend a pen torch pointing downwards one metre above the lens on nylon cord firmly anchored to the ceiling. Make the torch swing freely in various directions for about 30 seconds with the shutter open.

20.13 Through a moulded glass kitchen window

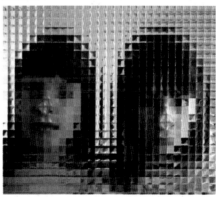

21 Using lens attachments

Attachments are sold which fit over your camera lens to produce various optical effects. Some soften detail, or split up the image; others are coloured *filters* which change the colour of all or part of your picture. Most attachments are best used on an SLR camera as you can then foresee their precise effect. If you use an advanced SLR set this to manual mode – attachments often confuse the camera's autofocusing.

Typically an effects attachment is a square or circular piece of clear plastic moulded or treated to alter the normal image formed by the camera lens. It is best slipped into a holder screwed onto the lens, Figure 21.3. Each attachment can then be rotated freely, or raised or lowered slightly, to suit a particular shot.

Some multi-image attachments have a number of parallel facets which repeat

21.2 Reeded glass attachment repeats a profile

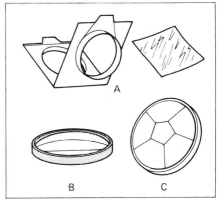

21.3 A. Holder for sheet colour filters (right) over lens. B. Half-lens close-up attachment. C. Multi-facet prism

21.1 The effect of one of many different types of starburst attachment

21.4 Using a three-facet prism attachment

one narrow strip of subject into a pattern. Strips may run vertically (Figure 21.2) or at any angle you choose to rotate the attachment. Other faceted units repeat whatever is centre frame three, four or more times around the sides of the picture. Multiple image attachments are best used with a subject having a strong,

simple shape and plenty of plain background. A starburst attachment is made in etched or moulded clear plastic. It spreads bright highlights in a scene into star-like patches, with radiating 'spokes' or 'points'. To make the starburst work use it for shots that include the direct sun, or contain many intense pinpoint highlights like Figure 21.1. Decorative lights at dusk, or sun reflected off rippled water take on a romantic, dream-like appearance. Some starbursts give each highlight six or so long spokes; others form spokes with refracted rainbow colours. Don't expect a starburst to work with softly lit scenes, however – it will simply have a slight diffusing effect.

If half your picture contents are very close to the camera and the remainder far away a semi-circular 'half lens' close-up attachment can render them both sharp, even at a wide aperture. In Figure 21.5 the camera lens was focused for the car but the attachment changed focus to the keys instead in the left half. You can just see

21.5 A half lens allows close and distant focusing at the same time

21.6 Darkening a blue sky. Left half no filter, right half using orange filter

the shift-of-focus line across the road and hedge, angled here at about 50°. Check appearance with the aperture preview button pressed – the smaller the aperture the more abrupt the change of focus. Be careful not to end up with pictures having two competing points of interest. Dozens of other effects attachments are made. Generally speaking the more exotic types are least used – results are overwhelming and soon lose their novelty.

Filters are attachments which all remove some light from the scene. A grey ('neutral density') filter just dims the image, useful for avoiding overexposure when you have fast film loaded but need an especially wide aperture or long exposure time. A pale colour filter will 'warm up' or 'cool down' the general mood of a scene. Both these and ND filters are available as 'graduates' – the colour or tone fading off in the lower half of the filter so you can just tint or darken the sky alone in landscapes. Stronger, overall colour filters compensate for fluorescent and other artificial lighting when using daylight-balanced film (essential for slide films, see Table, page 103).

Strong colour filters have a special role in black and white photography, allowing you to alter the normal translation of colours into monochrome. The rule here is that filters lighten the appearance of colours most similar to themselves; and darken their 'complementary' colours. (See colour wheel, page 54). For example, using a deep yellow, orange or red filter increasingly darkens blue sky, making white clouds stand out more clearly.

Most filters call for an increase in exposure. This is automatically taken into account if your camera exposure system reads light through the filter itself. If it does not, note the maker's suggested exposure factor (often printed on the filter as × 3, etc.) and over-ride aperture or shutter setting by this amount.

21.7 Effects of colour filtering in black and white

Filter	Effect on image
Orange	Darkens blue sky, green foliage. Lightens yellows, reds
Dark Green	Lightens green foliage Darkens blue sky, reds
Dark Blue	Lightens blue Darkens reds, yellows

22 Combining two exposures

A camera can allow you to combine two quite different scenes into one picture. This gives you the freedom to construct images which never existed in reality. Results can be bold and eye-catching like a poster, or strange and surreal, or perhaps make a statement which would be much less convincing if drawn. They may differ radically from normal vision, or at first glance look normal but contain something odd and disturbing (Figure 22.4). Some of these camera-based techniques involve exposing two pictures onto the same frame of film, or combining two pieces of slide film after processing. Others involve perfectly straightforward photography – but what is in front of the camera is not all that it may seem.

Sandwiched slides. 'Sandwiching' means placing two slide film images together in the same (glass) mount – details of one then appear in the lighter parts of the other. You can project your result, or send it for a colour print (instructing the lab to keep the sandwich together). Each slide

should be slightly pale – overexposed by about one stop – otherwise your sandwich will be too dark. It is worth keeping a selection of reject slides for this purpose.

Sometimes one existing slide suggests another which needs special taking to complete an idea. The sandwiched picture below, for example, started as an experimental night shot of a distant town, the camera being tilted downward and wiggled for the second half of a 4 second exposure. The result seemed to suggest chaos and stress. So another slide was shot of a man with his hands to his head and silhouetted in front of white sky. The silhouette was slightly overexposed so that when sandwiched it was not impenetrably black.

Figure 22.4 is also a sandwich, using two 'throwaway' slides. One shows the seashore with overcast white sky the other is just blue sky and cloud, but sandwiched *upsidedown* for surreal effect.

Projected slides. If you have a slide

22.1 Chaos and stress ....

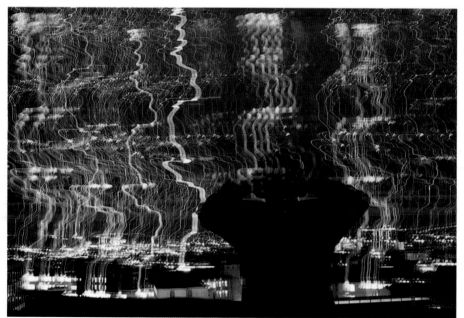

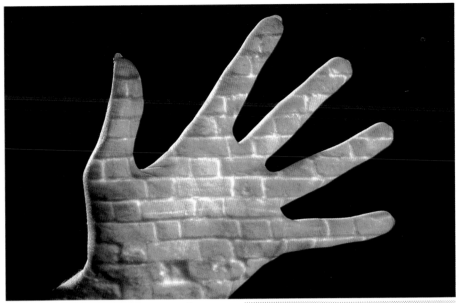

22.2 Slide projected onto a real hand

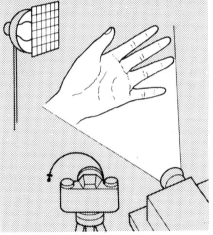

22.3 The set up for the result above

projector you can project one image onto a suitable light-toned object and photograph the result exactly as it appears to the eye. Work in a blacked out room with a bluish 80A filter on the camera to correct for the orangey light from the projector. In Figure 22.2 a slide of brickwork is projecting onto a hand. By using a distant, black background no brickwork appears elsewhere. A white card reflector (or another lamp) returned some general light from the rear, to give some form to the fingers and prevent them looking 'cut-out'. Correct exposure was measured off the hand alone. As this worked out at ¼ second at $f4$ the camera, hand, and projector all needed firm support.

Try projecting black and white negatives instead of slides. Your receiving surface can be eggs, paper cups, wooden blocks, or any object painted matt white for the purpose. Be careful not to make the result too complicated though – if the image you project has a strong pattern then pick a receiving object simple in shape.

22.4 Surrealism at the seaside

22.5 Is she there ... or not?

'B' two seconds were given, then the lens was covered with black card to allow the girl to go, and uncovered again for a further two seconds before closing.

The man looking two ways at once, Figure 22.6, is also two superimposed exposures; but he only moved his eyes (both) between each half, and this time the lighting was changed too, illuminating first one side of his face and then the other. Try this with open flash outdoors at night or in a darkened room. Lock the shutter open, fire a (separate) flashgun from arm's length on the right and then from arm's length, left. Finally, close the shutter. Give full exposure with each flash because they light quite different sides of the head.

PROJECTS

P22.1 By combining two or more images construct a photograph of a fantastic landscape.

P22.2 Produce a double profiled portrait, or show the contents of a household appliance inside its (opaque) container, by means of double exposure.

22.6 Lit one half at a time

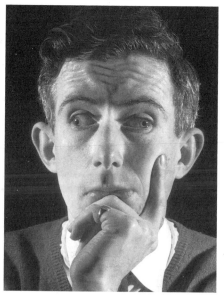

Double exposures. Unlike sandwiching slides, when you make one exposure on top of another the details of one picture appear in the *dark* parts of the other. The girl above for example purposely wore a dark dress and sat in a patterned chair. Using the camera on a tripod one half of the exposure was made. She then got up and carefully moved away, and the empty chair was exposed again onto the same frame of film.

Double exposures are easiest if your camera has a superimpose button. Otherwise work in a darkened room with slow film. Lock the shutter open on 'B' and either switch on the light briefly or fire a (bounced) flash, twice. Figure 22.5 was taken in dim domestic light requiring four seconds at *f* 16. Opening the shutter on

23 Manipulating prints

There is still plenty of scope for experimenting with images after you get your prints back from the processing lab. If you are good at handwork and have an eye for design there are the various possibilities of montage – pictures constructed from different paper prints arranged so that they join, overlap, or blend with each other. Your aim may be simply an original form of pattern and decoration, or the assembly of a panorama otherwise impossible to shoot 'straight' without special equipment. You can construct a picture of a crowd of people or a fantastic landscape, create a caricature or a visual pun.

Similarly the hand colouring of monochrome prints opens up possibilities of colour pictures in which every individual hue is under your control. Realistic or bizarre, coloured in full or limited to just a suggestion here and there, you have a free hand. In fact there is little point in aping regular colour photography – hand colouring is best used for interpretive effect.

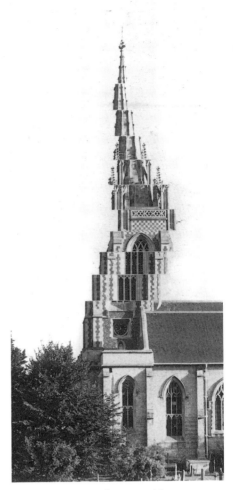

23.2 With slice-and-reassembly you can redesign any building

23.1 Four prints from the same negative make up a pattern montage

When your hand-worked print is complete you can copy it – either using your camera as shown on page 107 or through a high quality photo-copying machine. Results will then be free of joins or irregular surface finish.

Montage. A montage can combine elements or events which did not in fact occur together in real life. One person with eyes shut in a group can be pasted over with a cut-out print from another negative which is bad of everyone else. A strong foreground lead-in to a landscape

95

23.3 A hand-tinted black and white sepia toned enlargement. You need a set of photo colouring dyes

can be combined with a distant main subject, when they were really hundreds of miles apart and shot on different days.

On the other hand you can carefully dissect a single print into a regular pattern of slices, concentric discs, squares, etc., and then reassemble them in some different way, like the restructured architecture, Figure 23.2. In Figure 23.1 four prints have been butt-mounted to create one pattern. Look at the bottom left hand quarter only and you will find that the subject is simply the inside of a shed door, including the shadow of the handle. The lab supplied two normal prints and two printed through the *back* of the negative.

The landscape Figure 23.7 shows a more subtle form of repeat patterning – two butt-joined prints, one enlarged through the back of a negative and one from another negative, straight. Having the dog on only *one* half breaks up the symmetry of the final result, making you wonder if the scene is real or constructed. Pictures like this are best planned right from the start. They often work best when posing a question or expressing some point of view. Figure 23.4, for example, says something about the fact that we work with hard edges to our pictures, unlike scenes observed by eye. A print of the man was pasted onto a seascape print, and the shadow by his feet painted in with watercolour.

Colouring. Hand-tinting monochrome prints means that you can choose to leave some parts uncoloured and suppressed, others picked out strongly like the girl's eyes, Figure 23.3, irrespective of original appearance. Have your print made on fibre based paper (if possible make the print yourself and sepia tone it, see page 149). The print should be fairly pale because underlying dark tones desaturate your colours. Choose paper which is matt, not glossy – the latter's extra gelatin top coat often gives uneven results. Remember too that big prints take longer to colour than small ones. Begin with a size you know you can finish.

23.4 Montage (Courtesy Graham Smith)

Work with either transparent 'Photo-tint' dyes, or ordinary water colours. Dyes give stronger hues (you can build them up by repeated application) but unlike water-colours mistakes cannot be washed off. Start off by slightly damping your whole print surface to swell the gelatin, and firmly attach it on all four sides to hardboard with gummed brown tape. Work on the largest areas first, applying a colour wash on cottonwool. Medium small areas are then coloured in by brush (size 0–4).

Panoramas. A panorama can consist of two, three or more prints joined up to form one uninterrupted picture. This is a

23.5 Panoramas are a quick, cheap way of making a big picture of a scene you cannot get in completely with one shot. Include plenty of overlap

very successful way of showing an architectural interior or a landscape when you do not have a sufficiently wide angle lens. Building up a panorama also gives you an impressively large image from what were only quite small prints.

For the most accurate-looking result you must work carefully right from the shooting stage. Expose each picture for a panorama from exactly the same spot. Pick a viewpoint giving some kind of start and finish to your vista – perhaps trees at one end and a building at the other. Avoid showing objects close to you in the foreground and shoot with a 50 mm or longer focal length lens – otherwise it will

23.6 Avoid tilting the camera or pictures only join up in a curve (below).

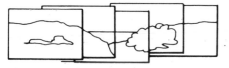

be difficult to join up both the near and the far parts of the prints. In any case overlap the contents of each frame by 30% so you need only use the central zone of each print.

Shoot your series of pictures as quickly as possible in case figure movements or fluctuating lighting conditions upset your results. A camera with motordrive will allow you to keep your eye to the viewfinder. If the panorama features a prominent continuous line, such as the horizon, keep your camera dead level. Pointing the camera slightly upwards or downwards results in prints that only join up to show this line curved (see Figure 23.6). Autoexposure cameras will make changes in settings if some frames forming a panorama contain larger dark areas than others. Prints will then show continuous elements too dark or light, and they will not match. Keep exposure unchanged by keeping to one manual setting or applying AE exposure lock.

Finally lay out your panorama prints overlapping so that details and tone values join up as imperceptibly as possible. Tack them down onto card with masking tape. Then, with a sharp blade, cut through each print overlap – either in a straight line or following the shape of

some vertical feature. Discard the cut off pieces and either tape together or butt mount the component parts of your panorama. If necessary trim or mask off the top and bottom as straight lines too.

Joiners. Not every set of panorama prints needs to marry up imperceptibly into one image. Another approach is to be much looser, abandon strict accuracy and aim for a mosaic which just suggests general

23.7 Constructed landscape

23.8 A mosaic type panorama, a contact sheet printed from carefully planned exposures on one complete 35 mm film. Always photograph from top left to bottom right

appearance. The painter David Hockney explored composite image-making this way by 'spraying' a scene with dozens of shots, often taken from more than one viewpoint and distance. The resulting prints, which he called 'joiners' both overlap and leave gaps. They have a fragmented jigsaw effect which suggests the passage of time and movement around the scene, concentrating on one thing after another.

Figure 23.8 is a rough mosaic in the form of a single sheet of contact prints. It was made by contact from a film of twenty consecutive exposures. The individual pictures, shot with hand-held camera and 50 mm lens, collectively make up something approaching a fish-eye view (see page 35). For this kind of result pre-plan how many exposures are needed per row. Don't overlap pictures – in fact compose trying to leave gaps where the black horizontal bars (perforations) will stretch across the final picture. The way that inaccuracies in a mosaic such as this re-structure the architecture gives it individuality and life, but try to pick a camera position giving a symmetrical view to help hold it all together as one picture.

PROJECTS

P23.1 Illustrate one of the following themes by means of a montage of prints: The Mob; Stairs and entrances; Family ties; Street-wise; Ecology rules!

P23.2 Shoot several interior scenes and landscapes, then use montage to combine the foreground of one with the background from another to give an inside/outside fantasy scene.

P23.3 Using three frames of film carefully shoot an accurate panorama showing part of the interior of your room. Then use all the rest of the film to shoot a loose 'joiner' of the whole room. Assemble and present the two results appropriately.

24 Setting up

A photographic studio is the rather grand term for any room you can clear enough space in to take pictures. Working in a studio should offer you full control over subject, camera position, lights and background, and is without doubt the best place to learn the basics of lighting and composition. A studio allows you time to experiment, especially with portraits or still life shots. Ideally you can keep essential bits and pieces on hand, and leave things set up. You can also shoot, check results, and if necessary retake the picture with improvements.

Your 'studio' may simply be an empty spare bedroom, or better still a garage, outhouse or barn. It should be blacked out so that all lighting is under your control.

In the studio shown below a large room has been cleared. Walls and ceiling are matt white and the floor grey, to avoid reflecting colour onto every subject. White surfaces are also important for 'bouncing' light when required. The window has a removable blind and the glass behind is covered with tracing paper. If daylight is needed for lighting it is therefore soft and diffused.

You don't need a lot of lighting units. Photographic lamps are of two main kinds – spotlights and floodlights (as described overleaf). They need to be mounted on height-adjustable floor stands and have tilting heads. The 'boom' stand below is an ideal way to position a lamp high up to backlight a figure or illuminate the back-

24.1 A room cleared to form a temporary studio. The table with curved card background is used for still lifes

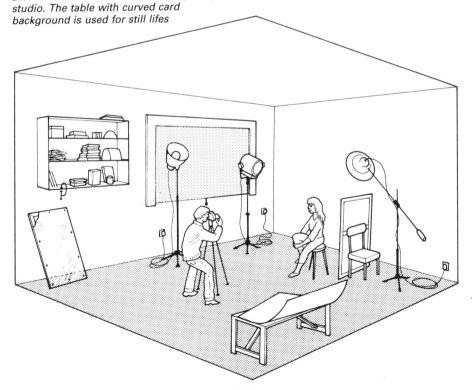

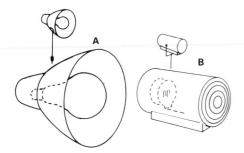

24.2 Basic studio lamps. A: floodlight giving soft, even lighting. B: spotlight giving hard lighting like direct sunlight. Its lamp focuses for narrow or wide beam

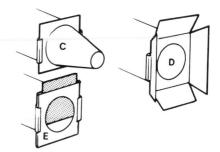

24.3 Attachments for spotlights C: Snoot and (D) Barndoors help to limit the light beam, shade camera from spilt illumination. E: Holder for coloured acetate filters

ground. You also need a stool for portraits and one or two reflector boards and diffusers. These can be made from white card, or tracing paper stretched over a simple frame. Have a table to support small still life subjects at a convenient height. You will also need lots of useful small items – sticky tape, string, blocks of wood to prop things up with, modelling clay, wire and drawing pins.

A *floodlight* is a general term for a source which gives even illumination, and causes solid objects to cast shadows with soft edges. Typically it has a 500 watt diffused glass bulb surrounded by a large, open reflector. A traditional desk lamp produces similar effects, although being much dimmer is suitable only for inanimate objects. A typical *spotlight* uses a small clear glass 500 watt lamp in a lamphouse with a moulded lens at the front. A lever shifts the lamp, giving light in either a narrow or broad beam. Various attachments help you to shade off parts of

the light. Spotlighting is harsh, causing sharp edged shadows, especially when set to broad beam. The nearest domestic substitute for a photographic spotlight is an integral reflector bulb, or you could use a slide projector.

Unless you only work in black and white, however, you must ensure that the light from all your lighting units matches in colour. 100 watt lamps, for example, give yellower (as well as dimmer) light than 500 watt lamps, so avoid using them together for colour photography. Then, having matched up your illumination, you can fit a camera lens filter if necessary (see table facing page) to suit the colour film you are using.

Another approach is to use flash in your studio, linking several flash units together and then shooting on unfiltered daylight type colour film. Flash heads for studio work often have built-in modelling lamps so that you can see their precise lighting effect.

25 Controlling lighting

Exploring lighting given the freedom offered by a studio is interesting and creative, but be prepared to learn one step at a time. Firstly, if you are shooting in colour, match up the colour balance of your film with the colour of your lighting as closely as possible. The table, right, shows the conversion filter needed over the camera lens for daylight colour film (print or slide) according to the type of light source you are using. A few colour films, mostly slide, are balanced for artificial light and so need different filtering.

Start off with a still life subject because it is easier to take your time experimenting with this than when shooting a portrait. Keep to one light source at first.

D/L Film	Light Source	Art. Film
None	Flash or Col. Match Tube	85B
80D	Warm White Fl. Tube	81C
80A	500 W Studio Lamp (3,200 K)	None
	100 W Domestic Lamp	82A

The aim of most studio lighting is to give a fairly natural appearance as if lit by the sun. This means having *one* predominant source of light and shadows, not two or three. It is also more natural positioned high rather than low down.

Set up your camera on a tripod and compose the subject. You can then keep returning to check appearance through the camera viewfinder for every change of lighting. Position your light source (a spotlight, for example) somewhere above camera height and to one side of the

25.1–2 Spotlight used alone and (right) with a large white card added on the right. Shadows become paler without forming additional shadows

A

B

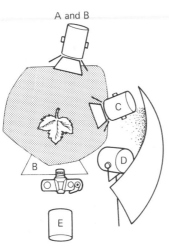

A and B

B

C

D

E

C

D

E

subject. Adjust it to give the best lighting direction for showing up form, texture, shape, etc. – whatever you consider most important to stress.

Be careful about contrast, the difference in brightness between lit and shadowed parts, at this point. Outdoors in daylight the sky always gives some illumination to shadows; but in an otherwise darkened studio direct light from a single lamp can leave very black shadows indeed. You may want to 'fill in' shadows with just enough illumination to record a little detail, using a large white card reflector as shown in Figure 25.2. This throws back very diffused light, and since it does not produce a second set of clearly defined shadows you still preserve that 'one light source', natural look.

The five studio shots, facing page, show some of the other changes lighting can make to subject appearance, especially texture. The drawing shows where the (single) light source was positioned for each version. In *A* the spotlight was positioned at the rear of the stone slab, a little above lens height. Its direct light exaggerates texture but gives such contrast that the film both overexposes highlights and underexposes shadows. Version *B* uses a reflector board close to the camera to return diffused light into the shadows, as with the paper chicken, Figure 25.2. In *C* the spotlight is still low but now to one side, changing the direction of the harsh shadows. For *D* the spotlight was turned away from the leaf and shone onto a large white card. The result is diffused ('soft') light, still directed from the side but now free of sharp edge shadows and even less contrasty than *B*. *E* shows the effect of using the spotlight direct, now positioned close to and directly above the camera. This frontal lighting is like flash on the camera – there is plenty of detail but it is like a drawing without shading, suppressing texture and form.

◄

25.3–8 Five ways of lighting a simple subject. Each gives a different appearance to texture and form

25.9 Lighting directed from below is unnatural – gives dramatic, 'theatrical' portraits

Arguably *B* gives the best compromise between drama and detail, although as a beginner you will often be tempted by *A* because it looks good in the studio. Always remember that your eye can cope with greater contrast than film will successfully record.

Soft, directional lighting (meaning diffused light from one side) like *D* is often a good basis for portrait lighting too. For the result in Figure 25.10 you can turn one or more lamps to illuminate a large part of the studio wall on the left. Then bring up a reflector board close on the right of the camera as fill-in.

25.10 Soft, directional light, created by illuminating the left hand studio wall, gives a natural effect

25.11–12 Right hand version here used a tiny cut out window shape in slide projector to suggest room setting

Like viewpoint and framing there are no absolute 'rights' or 'wrongs' of organised lighting. You must decide which subject features you want to emphasise or suppress, and the general mood you need to set. You can dramatise and dominate the subject matter with your lighting, or keep the light simple and subsidiary so that subject features alone make your shot. Look at the total change of feeling you can achieve when a face is lit unnaturally, from directly below (Figure 25.9).

All these are options and possibilities. Experiment until you can forecast and control how the final picture will look. Remember what you learnt by observing natural lighting outdoors. After all, a spotlight is like the direct sun and a flood like slightly hazy sun, except that you can

set their position instantly instead of waiting for different times of day. Again, bounced or diffused lighting has an effect similar to overcast daylight.

Using more than one light. As you get more experienced it becomes helpful to use more than one lighting unit at a time. Don't allow this to interfere with your main lighting though, destroying its 'natural light' basis of causing only one set of shadows. The second lamp might well separately illuminate the background behind a portrait or still life. This allows you to make the background lighter, or graduated in tone, or coloured (by filtering the light source). Again a second lamp might be needed to rim light someone's hair from behind, or just pick out one item among many. It can also break up large empty backgrounds by forming carefully controlled shadow patterns. In Figure 25.12 a slide projector was used to form a pattern on the far studio wall looking like a patch of sunlight from a window. The 'window bars' were tiny thin strips of black paper set between the glasses of a slide mount, and projected obliquely onto the wall. The musician, seated well forward of the background, was lit by floodlight bounced off a reflector board.

Lighting for copying. Photographic copying means accurately recording two-dimensional subjects such as artwork, photo-prints, montages and paste-ups, slides, and so on. You can turn prints into slides, slides into prints, or colour into

25.13 Methods of reducing light contrast without creating a second shadow

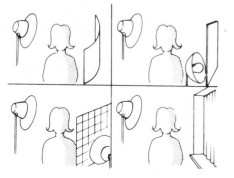

black and white. It is important, however, to light as evenly as possible, and have the camera set up square-on. Drawings, pictures and clips from papers are best taped against black cardboard, attached to the wall, and lit by two floodlights positioned about 30° to the surface. Keep each flood well back for even illumination. Check lighting with a pencil (Figure 25.14) held at right angles to the original. The two shadows should be equally dark, and together form one straight line.

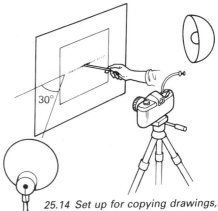

25.14 Set up for copying drawings, photoprints etc.

To copy a slide lay it horizontally on translucent opal plastic, masked along all four edges, with wide strips of black card. Illuminate the plastic from underneath using a floodlight (bounced off white card to avoid heat damage). Support the camera square-on and directly above, fitted with close-up extension tubes or bellows to allow a same-size image. Best of all use a slide copying attachment (Figure 25.15) added to an SLR fitted with tubes or bellows. The slide slips into the far end of the attachment, in front of a light diffuser.

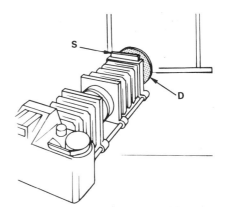

25.15 Slide copying S: Slide. D: Light diffuser. Bellows unit extends lens forward of camera body

Copying an image shown on a TV or computer screen does not require lighting equipment. Have the camera on a tripod, square-on to the screen. Darken the room, or set up a tunnel of black paper between camera lens and screen. For TV, shoot on unfiltered daylight type colour film at the aperture shown when the shutter is set to ¼ second. Shorter exposures give you a dark band across each picture. For best results shoot when the screen image features a static close-up.

25.17 Image photographed from TV screen

25.16 Avoiding camera reflection when copying computer display

PART EIGHT – BLACK AND WHITE PROCESSING AND PRINTING

26 Processing a film

Doing your own processing and printing allows you to have much more control over your results. You probably won't save money, but mastering the skills is enjoyable and will allow you to produce prints just the way *you* want them to look. This grows more important the further you progress in your photography – aiming for your own style of pictures or perhaps tackling specialised subjects beyond the range of the average commercial laboratory.

By far the best way to start is to process black and white film and make black and white prints (by contact and by enlargement). This will get you familiar with handling chemicals and setting up and working in a darkroom. Later you can progress to the extra challenge of judging colour test prints and working in the near darkness of a colour printing darkroom. Colour slide films are really not worth do-it-yourself processing. The cost of chemicals, rigorous temperature control needed, and the very limited manipulation of results possible mean that slide processing is best undertaken by automatic machines at a lab.

What you need. Processing black and white negatives is in many ways like cooking – you use liquids, and have to control time and temperature quite carefully. You also need some basic equipment. The eight most important items are shown below. (1) is a light-tight plastic tank containing a reel. You push or wind your film into the spiral groove of the reel in the dark; the whole length is held only along its edges, with each turn slightly separated from the next so that processing solutions act evenly over its entire surface. Each solution is poured in through a light-proof hole in the tank lid. You block off the hole and invert the tank occasionally to agitate the solutions; some tanks have a plastic rod to rotate the reel for the same purpose.

(2) Bottles containing developer and fixing solutions. A general purpose concentrated liquid developer such as Kodak HC-110 or D-76 (made up from powder) is best to start with. Made-up developer can be stored for weeks in a stoppered container. The acid hardener fixing solution is simpler and cheaper, and is also known by its main constituent 'hypo' (sodium thiosulphate). Unused fixer keeps indefinitely. Never let developer and fixer mix, because they will neutralise each other.

(3) A plastic graduate holding sufficient solution to fill your tank. Also have

26.1 Basic equipment for processing film

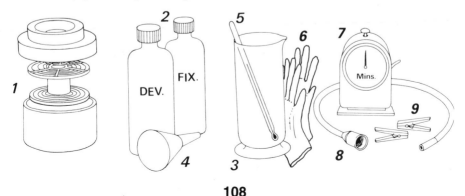

108

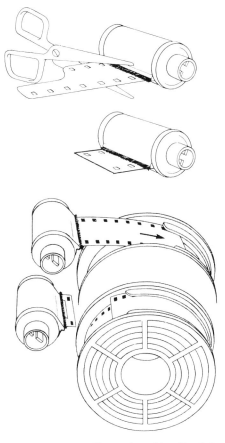

26.2 Trimming film end, and loading into reel

front of the film to give a square shape for loading. So when you rewind your exposed 35 mm film in the camera try to leave its tip protruding from the cassette, to allow you to trim it in the light, Figure 26.2.

The stage after this – winding a whole exposed film into the reel – only takes a few minutes but *must* be done in total darkness. If you don't have a darkroom use a large cupboard. It is also possible to untuck one side of your bed, pushing your hands in *deep* under the blankets in-between the sheets. Alternatively, buy a light-proof 'changing bag', Figure 26.3, which pushes onto your arms. Feed film in direct from the cassette (as shown left) or use a bottle opener to take off one end and withdraw the spool of film. The actual way the film slides into the reel grooves depends upon your particular make of tank. Some are cranked in, others just pushed. As soon as the whole film is loaded place the reel in the empty tank and fit on the lid. You can then do all your processing in ordinary lighting.

Using the solutions. The various stages and typical times of processing are shown in Figure 26.4. Developer solution, waiting in the graduate at the recommended temperature (normally 20°C) is poured in

(4) a plastic funnel for re-bottling solutions, and (5) a photographic thermometer clearly scaled from about 13°C (55°F) to 24°C (75°F). Other items are (6) thin plastic gloves for handling chemicals (see page 150); a minute timer (7); a flexible plastic tube (8) for ducting wash water down into your tank through the lid hole; and (9) plastic pegs to attach to top and bottom of your processed film when it is finally hung up to dry on a nylon cord.

Loading the tank. Before you use a tank for the first time practise loading with a scrap film or unwanted (and uncut) length of negatives. Do this first in the light, then with your eyes closed, then in a darkened room. It's important not to force and buckle the film during loading, or you may get results as shown on page 111. The shaped tongue must be cut off the

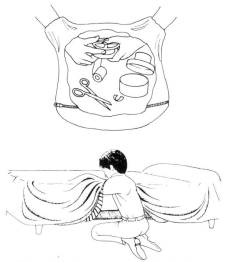

26.3 A changing bag, top, or just using your bed saves having a darkened room

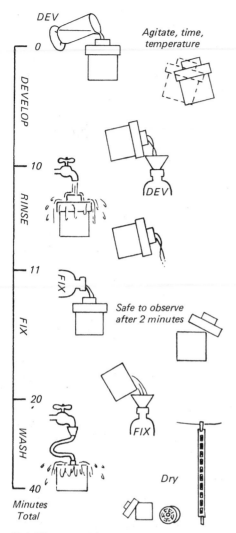

Agitate, time, temperature

DEV

Safe to observe after 2 minutes

Dry

Minutes Total

26.4 Film processing, stage by stage

the tank the creamy surface of your film now carries a black image corresponding to where it received light in the camera. For the next step, rinse, you fill the tank to overflowing with water and immediately empty it again. This helps to remove developer from the film. (Alternatively use 'stop bath' solution which halts development faster.)

Now fixer solution is poured into the tank and agitated. Fixer temperature is less critical than developer – room temperature is adequate. The fixer turns creamy silver halides unaffected by development into colourless compounds which can later be washed out of the film. Your film needs about 10 minutes in the fixer, but after 1–2 minutes most of the film's milkiness has cleared and you can remove the tank top without having light affect your results. When the film has finished its fixing time, the solution is returned to its bottle.

Next a twenty-minute wash in cold water removes all remaining unwanted chemicals and you can remove the processed film from the reel and carefully hang it up to dry, with a peg attached to each end. A few drops of photographic 'wetting agent' in the final wash water helps the film to dry evenly. Always hold film by its edges only. Once it has fully dried cut it into convenient strips of 5–6 negatives and immediately protect these in sleeves made for the purpose (see Figure 26.5).

and the clock started. The time required depends upon the developer and type of black and white film you are processing. You must regularly agitate the solution to avoid streaky development, typically by gently inverting the tank several times during the first 30 seconds, and then for 5 seconds every half minute. At the end of development time you pour the solution out through the light-tight tank top. It is either poured away (if 'one-shot' only) or returned to its bottle for re-use.

Although you cannot yet look, inside

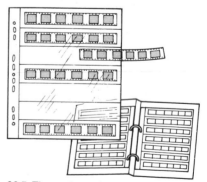

26.5 These sleeved pages hold strips of 35 mm processed negatives, fit into a ring binder

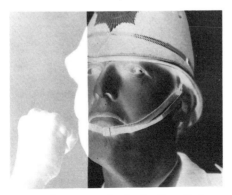

26.6–8 Some negative faults. Top: Dark, crescent-shaped kink marks. Centre: Undeveloped clear patch, where this part of the film remained in contact with another. Bottom: Section of all (or several) negatives shows pale picture, with straight line boundary. Can be caused by having insufficient developer in tank

Faults to avoid. Don't put the fixer in first – this will destroy all your pictures! Check temperatures before and during development, and be careful with timing, otherwise it is easy to under or overdevelop (see Figures 26.9–17). Avoid putting finger marks or splashes of any kind on your film – remember that it is particularly vulnerable to scratches, dust, hairs, etc., when drying.

If your film is clear with no images check to see if edge printing (name of film, frame numbers etc.) is present (see pages 78–9). If the information is there you have either processed an unused film or the camera was faulty – shutter not opening, or film not winding on. The edge data is printed by light, so if it is *not* present the fault is almost certainly processing. Perhaps the developer was totally exhausted, or solutions used in the wrong order? Totally black film has been badly fogged to light either before or during development.

Film which is still creamy has not been fully fixed, and patches of uneven tone usually means uneven development. Perhaps adjacent coils of film touched each other in the reel? Dark crescent shaped marks (Figure 26.6) and kinks or creases in the film itself are due to rough handling. The film was most likely buckled after removal from its cassette, when you were trying to load the reel in the dark.

Most of the time, however, faults are concerned with negatives that are a bit too dark ('dense') or too pale ('thin'). At first it is difficult to tell whether, say, a thin negative is due to underexposure or insufficient development. Of course, if every picture on your film looks thin the fault was probably development although it could also be mis-set ISO rating on the camera.

As Figures 26.7–15 show though, an *underexposed* negative is characteristically transparent and empty of detail in subject shadow areas, such as the girl's hair. A correctly exposed but *underdeveloped* negative shows more detail here, but looks generally weak and grey

111

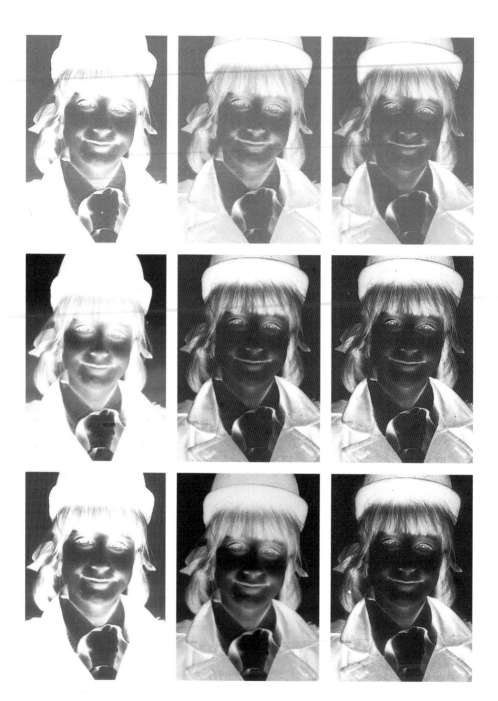

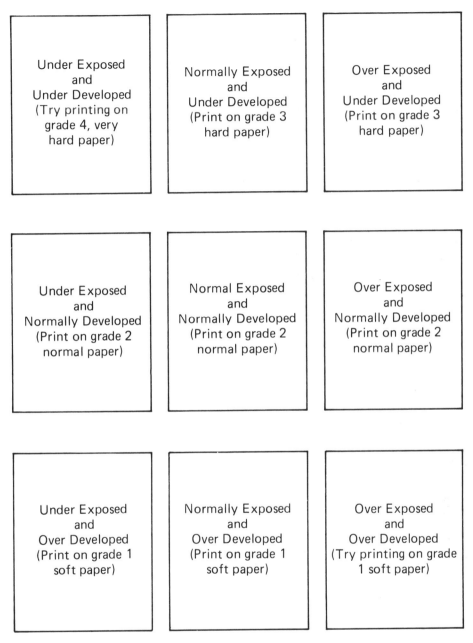

Under Exposed and Under Developed (Try printing on grade 4, very hard paper)	Normally Exposed and Under Developed (Print on grade 3 hard paper)	Over Exposed and Under Developed (Print on grade 3 hard paper)
Under Exposed and Normally Developed (Print on grade 2 normal paper)	Normal Exposed and Normally Developed (Print on grade 2 normal paper)	Over Exposed and Normally Developed (Print on grade 2 normal paper)
Under Exposed and Over Developed (Print on grade 1 soft paper)	Normally Exposed and Over Developed (Print on grade 1 soft paper)	Over Exposed and Over Developed (Try printing on grade 1 soft paper)

26.9–17 The effects of over and underexposure and development

('flat'). A dense negative due only to *overexposure* records the subject's lightest parts as so solid that finer details are destroyed. Notice how shadows have ample detail though. *Overdevelopment* instead gives a negative that is contrasty and 'bright' – dense in highlights but carrying little more shadow detail than a correctly developed film. See also Figures 6.1–3.

27 Contact printing

Film processing does not really require a darkroom, but before you can print or enlarge your negatives you will have to organize yourself some kind of blacked-out room to work in. This might have to be the family bathroom, quickly adapted for the evening (Figure 27.1). Maybe you can convert a spare room, or perhaps you are lucky enough to have use of a communal darkroom designed for the purpose at a school or club, as shown below.

The most important features to consider when you are planning either form of darkroom are: black-out; ventilation; water supplies and electricity.

Excluding the light. Existing windows have to be blocked off – either temporarily using thick black plastic or paper, or more permanently with hardboard. Alternatively buy a black fabric roller blind. The bathroom door may need strips of black plastic or draught excluder strip taped along its edges. As long as you have kept out unwanted light the walls of the room can be quite pale toned – a matt

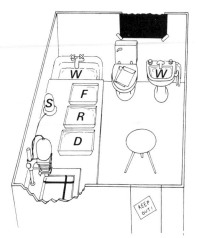

27.1 Darkroom in adapted bathroom. (For key to contents see Figure 27.2)

white finish helps to reflect around the coloured illumination from your safelight, and prevents dark shadows in corners.

Ventilation. One person working for an hour in the darkroom may not find the air too stuffy, but for groups working for longer times you need a light-tight air extractor fan (V). The school darkroom also uses a light trap instead of a door. This helps the circulation of air and makes it easy for people to enter or leave without disturbing others. Make sure that all wall surfaces inside the light trap are painted matt black, to reduce reflections.

Water supplies. In the bathroom use the bath to wash prints, and the hand basin to rinse your hands, etc., free of chemicals. The permanent darkroom has a large flat bottomed PVC sink specially made for photography. It holds trays for processing solutions, Figure 27.3, and a tank or tray for print washing stands in this at the far end. Always try to separate the wet stages of darkroom work from 'dry' work such as handling the enlarger and packets of paper, etc. In the larger darkroom each can take place on different sides of the room. In the bathroom however, where your 'bench' is just a thick board over the bath, the enlarger is next to the processing trays so take care to avoid liquid spills.

Electricity. Take special care over your electricity supply, needed for the enlarger

27.2 Purpose built school darkroom. D: Developer. R: Rinse. F: Fixer. W: Wash. S: Safelight. T: Towel. V: Ventilator. C: Clock with large second hand

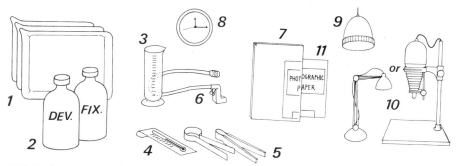

27.3 Basic equipment for contact printing.
Items described in text

and safelight, because electricity and water can be a lethal combination. Never let wires or switches come into contact with water or wet hands. Take your supply from a three-pin socket, and if possible include a circuit-breaker of the type sold for garden tools. Metal parts of your enlarger or safelight should be connected to the earth wire ('grounded'). If you are uncertain about any of your wiring get a qualified electrician to check it out. This is especially important in any board-over-the-bath bench arrangement. Remember that you are not allowed to have a permanent power socket outlet mounted in any bathroom. Take out any temporary wiring as soon as you have finished work, even though you intend to return within a few hours.

Print processing equipment. Most of the items necessary for contact printing are shown above, Figure 27.3. You need at least three plastic trays (1) big enough for your prints. 12"×10" is a good size. One is for developer, one for rinsing and washing, the other for fixing. Print developer (2) is similar to but much faster acting than negative developer. It comes as a concentrated solution, diluted just before use and discarded after your printing session. The fixer is a less concentrated form of negative fixer, and can be re-used.

You also need the measuring graduate used for films, and a photographic tray thermometer (blue spirit). The thermometer stays in the developer tray to tell you if

the solution is too hot or cold. (5) Plastic tongs – one for developer, the other only for fixer – allow you to keep your hands out of solutions. A washing hose (6) connects the cold water tap to the rinse tray and turns it into a print washing device. Have a clock to time minutes during processing and (if you have no enlarger timer) seconds during exposure.

Suitable orange lighting is permissible in the printing darkroom as black and white paper is not sensitive to this colour. You can buy a bench or hanging (9) safelight which contains a 25 watt bulb behind dyed glass, or use a standard strip light with a special coloured sleeve. The safelight is positioned near the developer tray (Figure 27.2) but no closer than specified, usually 1 metre (3 feet).

Exposing equipment. To expose your contact print you need an even patch of ordinary white light which will shine through the negatives laid out on the paper. You could use a reading lamp fitted with a 15 watt bulb, but as an enlarger will be needed later (page 120) for making enlargements this can conveniently provide your contact printing light. All you have to do at this stage is raise it to a height where it gives a large enough patch of light for your print as in Figure 27.4.

The negative strips can be held down in tight contact with the light sensitive printing paper during exposure by a sheet of thick glass, Figure 27.6. Better still buy a proper contact printing frame – glass

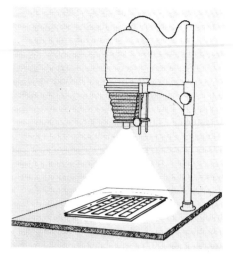

27.4 Exposing a contat print from a set of negatives

with thin plastic grooves on its underside to hold the film, and hinged to a baseboard.

Printing paper. Most black and white photographic paper is known as *bromide paper* due to the silver bromide used in its light-sensitive emulsion. It comes in different sizes, surfaces, types of base and grades of contrast. 10"×8" just accommodates seven strips of five 35 mm negatives. Start off with a packet this size of glossy, resin-coated, multigrade paper. (Later, when enlarging, you will need a set of simple enlarger filters to adjust the contrast of the paper, see page 121).

Printing a contact sheet

It is best to make a contact print from every film you shoot. This way you have a visual file of all your pictures, from which to choose the ones to enlarge. Prepare the solutions in their trays and bring the developer to its recommended temperature. Now you can change the lighting in your darkroom to safelighting and open your packet of paper. Position one sheet, glossy side upwards, under the switched off enlarger and re-close the packet. Lay out your negatives in rows on the paper with their emulsion (dull) side

downwards. Have all the edge numbers running the same way – it is irritating later to discover one row of pictures upsidedown. Then cover over the negatives with the glass.

With the enlarger near the top of its column and the lens aperture two f settings 'stopped down' from widest aperture, give a trial exposure of about 20 seconds. Remove the glass and put your negatives carefully to one side. As shown in Figure 27.5, slide the exposed sheet of paper smoothly under the surface of the developer. Note the time on the clock and rock the tray gently to keep the paper fully submerged. Magically the shapes of the frames on your film appear on the paper, then the pictures themselves – growing darker and stronger all the time. But keep one eye on the clock and remove the print when its recommended development time is up (typically 1 minute at 20°C for RC paper).

Maintain the same time in the developer no matter how fast or slowly the print darkens – in printing you alter results by *exposure*, and always keep development consistent. The print next has a quick rinse and goes face down into the fixer tray. Full fixing takes about 5 minutes although after one minute or so you can switch on normal lighting. In the example right (Figure 27.7) the exposure given is correct for most pictures on the sheet. If results were too *dark* you would give a shorter exposure time or reduce the lens aperture; if too *pale* increase exposure time or widen the aperture.

Prints can be allowed to accumulate in the fixer – for up to half an hour if necessary – before you put them to wash as a batch. Washing also takes about 5 minutes but keep separating the prints now and again, and prevent any floating face upwards to the surface where washing will be ineffective. After washing, sponge off surplus water from the front and back surfaces and dry your print by pegging it on a line or laying it out on blotting paper. RC plastic paper dries quickly but can be hastened with warmed air from a hair dryer.

116

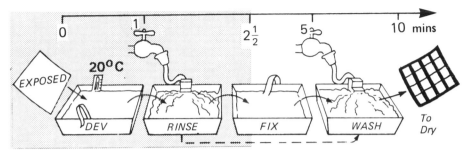

27.5 Print processing, stage by stage

Often you find that when exposure is correct for some pictures on the sheet it is too much or too little for others, because your negatives vary. This has happened in Figure 27.7 where the four frames at the bottom left are underexposed. You could make two sets of contacts, one exposed for dark pictures, one for light. But better still use a shaped card (Figure 27.8) to give 50% extra exposure time to this corner of the sheet. Look at Figure 27.9 to see the improvement. Note too that an ordinary wooden ruler is about the same width as 35 mm film. You can cover up individual rows or parts of rows of pictures by laying rulers on top of the glass, and then remove them according to the exposures required.

Number the contact sheet on the back with the same reference number you put on your set of negatives. Check carefully with a magnifying glass to see which images are sharp enough to enlarge, what people's expression look like, whether the composition works, and so on. With a white grease pencil or black felt pen you

27.6 Stop down the lens for the first, trial exposure

27.7 The result – correct for most, but not all, pictures

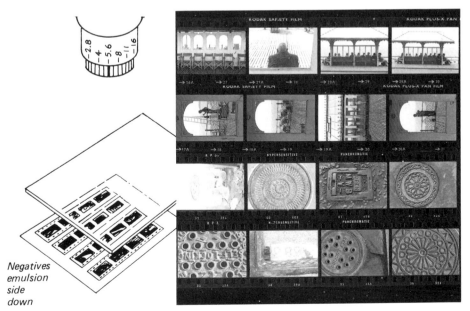

Negatives emulsion side down

117

can write on the print surface, marking up the best shots, and working out possible cropping.

Tips and suggestions. If your fingers get wet with chemicals *always* rinse and dry them before touching exposing equipment or dry photographic materials. Otherwise – even if it is just water – you will produce marks on prints (see page 128). Wear thin plastic disposable gloves if you wish to avoid all hand contact with solutions (although chemicals for black and white prints are no more toxic than many household products).

You may prefer fibre base paper instead of RC (plastic) type for contact printing and enlarging. Bear in mind however that fibre paper requires longer processing and washing times. Some people vary their development time, pour warm developer on light parts of the print, etc., to 'save'

results – but don't try doing this until you have a lot of experience. Control printing by varying exposure, not development – otherwise you will get very confused.

Colour negatives can be contact printed to give black and white results in just the same way as monochrome negatives, but often need about 2–3 times the exposure time. Similarly you can contact print a drawing to get a negative image on paper. The fir cone, Figure 27.11 started as a black pencil sketch on thin drawing paper, exposed under glass in face contact with photographic paper. Remember that results printed this way will appear reversed left-to-right, too. Pictures (called 'photograms') are also possible from the shadows of objects arranged directly on the surface of printing paper and exposed to light (see page 129).

27.8 *Shading to correct uneveness in a set of contact points*   27.9 *Corrected version of Figure 27.7*

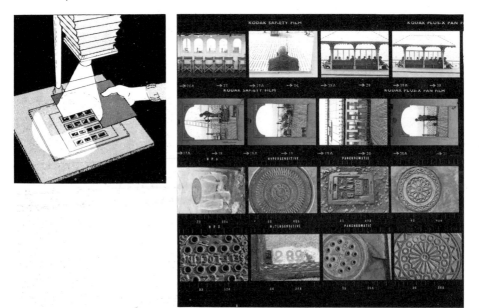

27.10 A contact sheet marked up for enlargements

27.11 Right. Contact printed from a pencil drawing on thin paper

28 Enlarging

Making an enlargement reveals details and gives an impression of 'depth' to your pictures which is lost in a small print. During enlarging too you can decide to exclude parts of the negative in order to improve composition; darken or lighten chosen local areas of the picture; and juggle with contrast and density so that (within limits) you can compensate for negatives which are slightly dark or pale. It is even possible to construct pictures with the enlarger, by combining parts of different negatives into one print.

The enlarger. Up to now the enlarger has just been a handy source of light for contact printing, but before making enlargements you need to understand it in more detail. Basically an enlarger is like a slide projector, although it has a much less powerful lamp and is attached to a vertical stand. Inside, to ensure that your negative is evenly illuminated, the light first passes down through large condenser lenses, or a plastic diffusing screen. The negative itself is held flat, emulsion side downwards, between two halves of a carrier which has a rectangular cut-out just large enough for the light to pass through one film frame. The negative carrier pushes into a slot in the enlarger just below the condensers or diffuser (see right).

Below the negative is a lens (typically 50 mm focal length) which you can move up or down to focus a sharp image on the enlarger baseboard. Adjustable bellows prevent the escape of any light between carrier and lens. An enlarging lens needs no shutter but has an adjustable aperture, usually scaled in *f*-numbers. Changing from one *f*-number to another doubles or halves the brightness of the image. (As you can feel and hear the position of each setting by a 'click' it is unnecessary to keep peering at numbers.) Your enlarger may contain a filter drawer in the lamphouse, as shown right, to accept contrast-changing filters for variable contrast ('multigrade') paper. Alternatively a filter

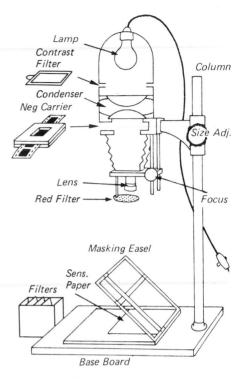

28.1 Parts of the enlarger

holder can be attached to the lens. The purpose of filters is explained on page 121.

The whole enlarger head can be moved up or down a firm metal column and locked at any height to control the *size* of enlargement. On the baseboard you will need a masking easel, which has a white base surface and a hinged frame with adjustable metal strips. You can move the easel around to compose your enlargement, adjusting the strips to give a picture of the chosen size and proportions. During exposure the bromide paper is held down flat and correctly positioned under the strips on all four sides. The strips also prevent light reaching the paper and so give your enlargement neat white borders. Avoid holding paper down by glass – this upsets sharpness as well as increasing the likelihood of dust specks and scratch marks.

If possible have an enlarging exposure timer – a clock switch which plugs in between enlarger and power supply. You set the estimated number of seconds needed, press a button, and the lamp switches on for exactly this time. Another useful aid is a focusing magnifier, a unit to magnify a small part of the image. You place this on the masking easel and look through it whilst focusing the enlarger.

The printing paper. For enlarging you use the same light-sensitive paper as for contact printing. In other words it can have a plastic RC base and so be a fast processing and drying type, or a fibre base (better for retouching, colouring and montage). The surface may be glossy, or semi-matt (again better for later handwork on the print). You can control the *contrast* of your enlargement – normal, hard, soft, etc. – in two ways. Either buy packets of grade 1, soft; grade 2, normal;

grade 3, hard, etc., or instead use one packet of variable contrast paper and buy a range of filters to tint the enlarger light. Using graded papers means you must buy several packets at once and possibly run out of a particular grade. Variable contrast ('Multigrade') paper is therefore more economic, once you have bought your filters. In addition you can make prints which differ in contrast between one chosen part and another (see page 127).

Making a test print. Start by picking a negative which has plenty of detail and a good range of tones. As shown in Figure 28.2, set the masking frame for your size of paper. Position the negative dull side downwards so that the shot you want to enlarge fills the cut-out part of the carrier. Push the negative carrier into the enlarger. Fit a filter for grade 2 (normal contrast) if you are using variable contrast paper, and open the lens aperture fully. Switch on the enlarger and change the darkroom from ordinary light to safelighting. You can now focus the projected image on the

28.2 Enlarging. Top sequence: making exposure test strip, see result overleaf. Bottom row: making final enlargement, shown page 123

TEST

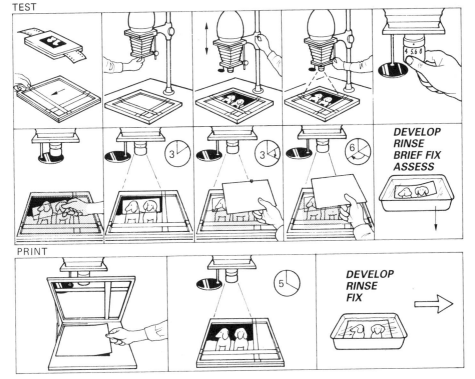

PRINT

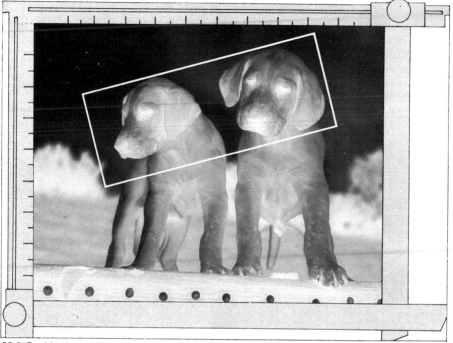

28.3 Positioning of the test strip

white easel surface, making further adjustment to enlarger height if necessary until your picture is exactly the right size, and sharp. Close down the lens aperture by about two clicks (three clicks if the negative is pale, or one if rather dense). Switch off the enlarger.

Cut or tear part of a sheet of your printing paper to form a test strip, and lay it face upwards on the easel where it will

28.4 Processed series of test exposures – the right-hand version gives most information

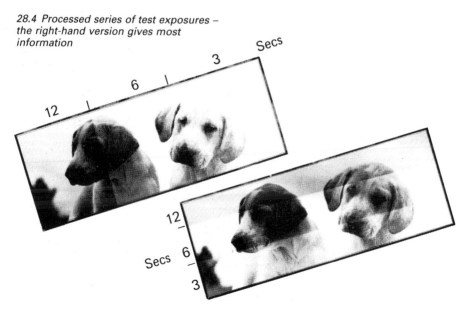

28.5 The final enlargement

receive an important part of the image (the puppies' heads in Figure 28.3). Now, by shading with a piece of card, you are going to give the paper three different exposure times, in strips as shown in Figure 28.2. Think carefully though, which is the most informative way for each strip of exposure to run. For example, if arranged as shown in the left hand test print of the puppies you will only find out how the longest exposure affects one puppy and the shortest exposure the other. But when each band is run longways instead you discover how much each exposure time affects both dogs' heads.

To get this result the whole test piece of paper was first given 3 seconds. Then, holding thick card an inch or so above it, two-thirds of the paper received 3 seconds more. Finally the card was shifted to give the final third another 6 seconds. The combined effect was therefore to give strips of 3, 6 and 12 seconds. By holding the card quite still a noticeable line of tone change records on the print, which helps you pick out the different exposure

bands when you judge results.

The test strip is processed in the same way as the sheet of contacts, page 117. You can then switch on normal lighting to decide which is the best exposure (if they are all too pale make a further test using longer exposure times, or a wider lens aperture if you prefer). With the puppies picture an exposure time of about 5 seconds was judged to look best. A whole sheet was then given this exposure, and when processed produced the result, Figure 28.5.

Controlling print contrast. If you look along the middle row of pictures on page 124 you see what happens when a normal contrast negative is printed onto different contrast grades of paper. On grade 1 paper (or variable contrast paper printed through a grade 1 filter) you get more greys between pure black and white than when using grade 3 paper (or a grade 3 filter on variable contrast paper). Grade 1 is your best choice when you are printing a contrasty negative like the one in the bottom row. Similarly you might use

28.6–17 Low, normal, and high contrast negatives printed onto . . .

. . . grade 1 (soft) paper

grade 3 for a flat, low contrast negative. In other words *contrast grade compensates for negative contrast*. Although not shown here, you can buy other graded papers.or (especially) use further filters for variable contrast paper, to give more extreme grades 0 or 4.

To get the best out of a set of negatives expect to use at least three different contrast grades, or filters. Even with the most accurate film processing the range of subjects recorded on any one film means that differences in lighting and subject tone range are bound to result in negatives of differing contrasts. The usual way to decide which grade to use is by simply examining the contrast of the image projected on the white surface of

... grade 2 (normal) paper

... grade 3 (hard) paper

your masking easel, and comparing it with how previous negatives have printed.

Don't expect miracles, however, when your film exposing technique has been faulty. If you look back again to the range of negatives on page 112 you will see some very pale and flat results because of underexposure and underdevelopment, and other dark negatives caused by over-exposure and overdevelopment. These are too lacking in either shadow or highlight details to be correctable by any contrast grade in printing.

Another reason for grades is to inten-tionally distort contrast. This may just be to give extra 'punch' and emphasis. Most of the pattern pictures on page 56 for

28.18 A 'straight' print, given 10 secs exposure, shows washed out sky although the land detail is reasonably correct

28.20 In this version an additional 12 secs given to the sky – making 22 secs total here – prints in missing detail

example, were printed using grade 3 or 4 to give extra strength. Strictly Figure 11.4 is not a 'correct' print – direct comparison with the subject would show you how tones have been increased in contrast – but the need here is for impact in the pattern.

28.19 Printing-in sky detail

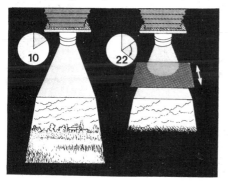

Printing-in, and shading. Since a longer exposure gives a darker print it is possible to give extra exposure time to just part of the paper where you want to darken your picture. You can use this 'printing-in' technique to bring up detail in a pale sky, like Figure 28.20 above. Of course, such details have to be present in the negative in the first place but often cloud information is quite dense on the film and sky records as white paper when you give your whole print correct exposure for ground details. The left hand print above had 10 seconds all over. The right hand version had the same but then the sky alone was exposed for a further 12 seconds while a card was used to stop light reaching the landscape part.

Unlike the making of test strips, you do not normally want a sharp edge line to show where change of exposure has taken

126

place. So while you are printing-in blur the line by keeping the card continuously on the move and holding it nearer to the lens than to your paper. If you use variable contrast paper it's also possible to change filters between the main and printed-in parts of the exposure. In this way landscape ground information can be printed grade 2 contrast, but dense, low contrast sky detail printed-in grade 4.

Printing-in an entire sky is a useful technique but you will even more often want to darken some relatively small, isolated part of a picture – the over-lit side of a face perhaps, or the window part of a room interior. The best way to do this is to give your printing-in exposure with a card carrying a hole about the size of a small coin. For the opposite effect – making an isolated central area *paler* – use a small disc of card taped to a thin but rigid piece of wire. You can then push this 'shader' into the enlarger light beam a few inches above the paper during part of the main exposure, to keep back light from the area that prints too dark.

The enlargement, below left, was just given an overall exposure of 14 seconds. The result looks correct over most of the image, but the dog's mouth is too dark and its hindquarters too light. The second version, shown below right, also received 14 seconds but during this time a disc-on-wire shader was pushed into the light beam about 2–3 inches above the paper, and allowed to cast a shadow over the

28.21 Shading and printing-in technique
28.22 (below left) Straight print
28.23 (below) Corrected print

28.24 Print from unsharp negative

28.25 Unsharp print from sharp negative

28.26 Hair and debris on negative

28.27 Damp fingermarks, solution splashes

open mouth for 3 seconds. Then, when 14 seconds was completed, a card with a hole in it about the same size as the disc was used to give extra exposure to the dog's hindquarters only, for another 5 seconds. In each instance the shader and the printing-in card were kept slightly on the move.

Print faults to avoid. If your printing paper still just looks white after processing or carries a ghost-like pale image, you may have processed an unexposed sheet, or exposed it upsidedown, or put it in the fixer first . . . or it may simply be grossly underexposed. Perhaps your developer is exhausted, contaminated, or much too diluted? If the print goes black all over including its white borders it was fogged to light – maybe the safelight is too bright, or someone has opened the packet in room lighting. If the borders remain white the fault is probably gross over-exposure, or perhaps light is reaching the easel other than through the enlarger lens?

A yellowish all-over stain suggests that your print was very over-developed (possibly in exhausted developer) or has not yet fixed properly. Uneven purplish patches are due to uneven fixing, for example, prints left face up and allowed to float to the surface of the fix solution.

Your print may show smears or blobs of darker or lighter tone (Figure 28.27) not present on the negative. The most likely cause is odd spots of water or developer getting onto the paper before processing. Perhaps your 'dry' bench was splashed with liquid or you handled dry paper with wet fingers? White specks, or hairs and other clear-cut squiggle shapes like Figure 28.26 are often debris on the negative – although sometimes due to dirt on the enlarger condenser which only appears clearly at a small lens aperture.

If your enlargement is not quite sharp check closely to see if the grain pattern of the negative has printed sharply; if it has (Figure 28.24) then the image shot in the camera was unsharp. But if the grain is also unsharp your enlarging lens is improperly focused. Sometimes a print from a perfect negative reveals a double image, over the whole picture or just some part you have printed-in. This is because you jogged the enlarger or paper part-way through exposure.

Unusual effects. Shading and printing-in also allow you to combine parts of several negatives into one picture. For Figure 28.29, for example, the mouth negative was first enlarged and exposed, shading the child's tongue and bottom left quarter of the picture the whole time. Then the negative was changed and the unexposed parts of the paper exposed to the train shot, this time shading the top and right hand side of the paper.

Photograms are worth exploring too. For Figure 28.30 below the enlarger was set as if for contact printing, but instead of negatives, chocolate buttons were just scattered on the surface of the paper. Then, after giving half the exposure time needed for a good black, all the buttons were shifted around and the same time repeated. Figure 28.28 goes further, using three pressed leaves in a pile on the paper.

28.29 One print from two negatives

One leaf was carefully removed after 3 seconds and another after 6 seconds of a 9 second exposure. After processing, this *negative* print was contact printed face down under glass onto another sheet of paper to give a *positive* result.

28.28 Print from photogram of leaves

28.30 Chocolate button photogram

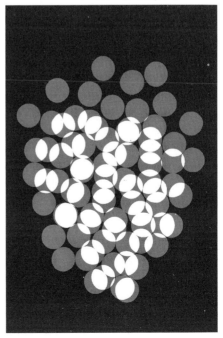

29 Finishing off

The final stage of photography is to present your results in the most effective possible way. If you made your own prints they must first be dried and finished; but even if you have received back work from a processing and printing lab several decisions still have to be made. Shots need to be edited down to your very best; cropped finally to strongest composition, and then framed as individual pictures or laid out as a sequence in an album or wall display. Slides can similarly be edited and prepared for projection. Finally negatives, slides and contact prints deserve protective storage and a good filing system, so that you can locate them again when required.

Drying prints. The simplest way to dry your washed prints is to first wipe off surplus water with a sponge or a flat (window-cleaning type) squeegee. Then peg them on a line, or lay them face up either on clean blotting paper or muslin stretched on a frame (see Figure 29.1). Special hot-air dryers are made which accept RC black and white paper and all colour papers. They give you dry results in a few seconds, but even when left at room temperature these plastic papers dry within about 15 minutes. If you have made black and white prints on fibre base paper, which is more like drawing paper, peg them up in pairs back-to-back to avoid curling.

Mounts and mounting. If your finished print is to be shown mounted with a border choose this carefully because pictures are strongly affected by the tone or colour of their immediate surround. Compare the two identical prints, Figures 29.2–3; on a *white* mount dark parts such as the shadows form a strong comb-shape, whereas on a black mount it is the pools of sunlight that become emphasised instead. Even a thin white border left from the masking easel can change the picture by enclosing and separating it from a dark mount – just as a black edge-line drawn on it would do the same on the white mount. Don't overdo coloured mounts or they may easily dominate your pictures. Colour prints often look best against a mid-grey, or a muted colour surround in harmony with the picture. If the dominant colour scheme of the shot is, say, green, try a grey-green mount.

If you have no special equipment to attach your print to its board use a double-sided adhesive sheet, or coat the back of the print with a spray adhesive (working in a well-ventilated place). Simpler still, attach the print to the mount along the one edge with masking tape and then secure a cut-out 'window mat' on top (see Figure 29.4). Use a firm, really sharp blade when cutting the window – make sure corners are left clean and free from bits. For the cleanest, flattest most professional look-

29.1 Drying prints by (A) muslin rack, (B) line and peg, or (C) hot air RC dryer

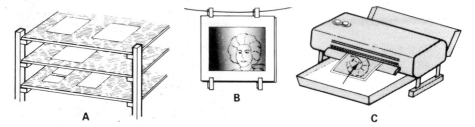

ing mounted result it is difficult to beat *dry-mounting*. You need access to a dry mounting press and electric tacking iron. As shown in Figure 29.5, there are four main steps. (A) Cover the back of your print with an oversize sheet of heat-sensitive mounting tissue. Brush over the centre of the tissue with the heated iron, to tack them together. (B) Trim print and tissue to the exact size you need. (C) Position your print accurately on a good quality board and carefully lifting each print corner tack the tissue to the board. Hold down the print centre with your other hand to prevent it moving during tacking. (D) Cover your print and board with a sheet of non-stick silicon release paper, insert the whole sandwich into the heated press and close it for about 15 seconds.

The mounting press should be set to the recommended temperature for your mounting tissue. This may be between 66°C and 95°C, according to type. Should the print not be fully attached to the board give a further, shorter period in the press.

29.4 *Print taped to card and covered by window mat*

If the tissue is firmly attached to the board but not the print, or the print is blistered, your press was too hot.

Spotting. Sometimes otherwise perfect enlargements show one or more tiny white dust specks. Spot these in with black watercolour applied almost dry on the tip of a size 0 brush. Checking through a magnifier, stipple tiny grey specks into the white area until it dis-

29.2–3 *Picture appearance can be affected by light or dark tone of mount*

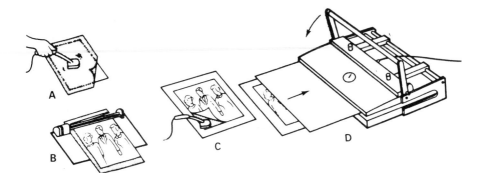

29.5 Stages in dry mounting. A: Tacking
tissue to print. B: Trimming. C: Positioning
and tacking on mount. D: Placing in heated
press

appears. Grey is successful for colour
prints too.

Print sequences and photo-essays. If you
have shot some form of narrative picture
sequence you must decide the minimum

29.6–13 Story sequence

number of prints needed to tell your story. Perhaps the series of pictures was planned right from the start, set up and photographed like scenes from a movie. Sometimes though it evolves from part of a heavily photographed event or outing, which becomes a narrative story once you begin to sort out the prints.

The sequence below is of this evolutionary kind – often the only way of making a documentary type story (one which relates to actual events). In this case all the dog pictures were taken first and edited down to seven, then picture number 6 shot specially to fill a gap in the story. You can help continuity by trimming all your prints to the same shape and size. Then present them in rows on one mount (as here) so that they read like a cartoon strip, or run them one to a page in a small album or a hand-made book.

You may want to caption such pictures, but be sparing in what you write. As a photographer it is often best to let your pictures speak for themselves, even though some viewers may differ slightly in the story they read from the sequence. People don't like to have ideas rammed into their heads; unless you can write brilliant copy you will probably only be repeating what can be seen anyway. It's easy for the result to seem precious or patronising.

Sets of pictures may share a theme but,

29.14 Part of a documentary series on the town of Reading. Differing print sizes give variety

29.15 Using L-shaped cards to decide trim

because they are not based on a narrative to be read in a set order, allow you much greater freedom of layout. Follow some of the layout ideas on the pages of picture magazines and display your work as a 'photo-essay', using half a dozen prints to an exhibition board or large format album. As Figure 29.14 shows, you can make all the picture proportions different in a documentary series, to give variety and best suit each individual composition. Using L-shaped cards on the enlargement (or contact print) helps you to decide the cropping.

Don't be tempted to slip one or two dull or weak pictures into a photo-essay just because their subject content ought to be included. Every shot should be good enough to stand on its own; if necessary take some more pictures. Similarly if one print is a bit too small or large relative to others be prepared to print it again at a different size. When laying out your set take care over the way you relate one print to another – the lines and shapes

they contain should flow together well, not conflict and confuse.

Albums and files. Smaller family albums give you less scope for layout ideas but they are a quick, convenient way to sort out your best shots. Most albums are geared to standard shop enprints, two or three to a page. The type which have a clingfilm overlay to each page allow you to insert, re-position or remove prints at any time without adhesive or mounting equipment. A pocket file, Figure 29.15, is also a handy way of carrying around small prints.

Unframed enlargements on individual board mounts are most safely stored in boxes. You can keep to one standard mount size and buy or make a box which opens into two halves so that anyone viewing your pictures can move them from one half to the other.

Don't overlook the importance of filing negatives and contact prints efficiently too – otherwise you may spend hours searching for an important shot you want

enlarged. A ring file with loose-leaf sleeved sheets each accepting up to 36 negatives is ideal. If you make a contact sheet off all your pictures punch each one and file it next to its set of negatives (see page 110).

Slides. Processed slides are normally returned to you in plastic, glassless mounts. For maximum protection from fingermarks and scratches it is advisable to transfer your best slides into glass mounts. If you have your own projector these selected shots can be stored in a magazine, ready for use. Each slide should have a large spot stuck on its mount at the bottom left when you hold the picture correct way up, exactly as it should look on the screen. Then it is always loaded into the projector with this spot *top right* facing the lamp.

Remember when you project slides to use a matt white screen (even a slightly tinted wall will distort colours). Ensure that the room has a full blackout too. Slight presence of light will have a

135

29.16 Presenting prints. Left: Album with clingfilm page overlays. Right: Print box. Centre: Glass-fronted frame and pocket file

decisive effect on the darker parts of your pictures, dulling colours and turning blacks into flat greys. If you have a large slide collection store them in numbered clear plastic sheets (Figure 29.17) which each hold 24 slides and hang in any standard filing cabinet.

Photo-CD. If you don't have a projector another good way of group viewing your pictures is to use a photo-CD player and the domestic TV. Have the lab make a CD of your shots (taken on negative or slide, colour or black and white) up to 100 per disc. The player's remote controller will memorise any series of favourite pictures you choose, so that different 'programmes' (photo-essays, sequences, etc.) can be replayed to order, although only seen one picture at a time. Most players also offer a frame button which brings up a white rectangular outline on the screen you can move around. The image in this frame then blows up to full screen size without loss of quality, when you press a tele button. You can also videotape your CD programmes of pictures and then send tapes to people instead of prints.

29.17 Slides. Left: Spot on slide mount should be top right (image upside down) when loading projector. Right: Clear plastic hanging sheets have individual pouches for slides, can be numbered for filing

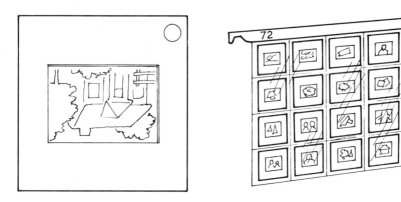

30 Assessing your photography

It is important to learn how to assess your progress in picture making. One approach is to put prints up on the wall at home for a while and see if you can keep on enjoying them – perhaps seeing something new each time you come back to look. Another way is to discuss your pictures with other people – photographers and non-photographers. Discussion is easiest if you are a member of a group, or club or class, putting up several people's latest work and then getting everyone to contribute comments. At worst it allows you to see your own pictures afresh and also discover what other people have been doing. At best you can get down to learning why pictures are taken and what reaction and influence they have on others.

But how do you criticise photographs, deciding what is 'good' and what 'bad'? There are at least three approaches:

(1) Technical quality. Is the exposure and focusing correct? Could the print have better colour; be darker or less contrasty; is there too much grain? This form of criticism is useful to improve your technical ability. It is particularly valid in photography used for record making and is mostly concerned with facts (the negative is either sharp or unsharp, grainy or fine grain). The danger is that you apply the same rules to every picture irrespective of subject and approach. Some photographs more concerned with expression *should* be dark and grey or light and contrasty, to strengthen and carry through the particular image.

(2) Function and purpose of the shot. Establish (or imagine) why the picture was taken, and then decide whether the photographer has succeeded in this visual intention. Maybe he or she was interested in a particular pattern, or wanted to communicate the relationship between two people. Perhaps the picture is making a broader comment on society in general . . . or captures the peak of some action or event.

(3) Is it well structured as a picture? Maybe its main strength is in its design and structure, the actual subject itself being unimportant (Figure 9.4); or perhaps the subject is the most important element because of its attractiveness or drama. Again, most of the interest may be in what can be read *into* a picture – Figure 5.6 or 22.1, for example.

Whatever approach to criticism you adopt (and they can all be used at once) your photograph is a means of communication and a sort of catalyst. On the one hand you the photographer with your own attitudes and interests, and the physical problems you remember overcoming to get this result. In the middle the photograph, which may or may not put over facts and ideas. On the receiving end the viewer with his or her interests and background experience, the way they feel at that particular moment and the physical conditions under which the photographs are seen.

Discussing *photography* as well as *photographs* is very much a part of studying the subject. What things can photography do well, and what can painting or drawing do better? How many ways might a particular theme or type of subject be approached? Look at the work of other photographers, in exhibitions and collections of their work printed in books. Notice too the photographs in current newspapers and magazines – clip out and keep on file published editorial and advertising pictures that really work for you and use these as discussion points too.

31 How photography is used

Photography is a medium, like writing or speaking, for communicating ideas and information. In the hands of an artist it can express personal feelings with almost as much freedom as drawing or painting. Used by a scientist it can report and measure in a factual way. Everyone can use photography today in their own way to make interesting images and visual notes, for it has become one of the most universal forms of illustration.

It's hard to believe that 70 years ago most newspapers and magazines appeared without photographs, having instead illustrations drawn on metal looking rather like the engraving on page 8. Great news events had to be described in words, or drawn from uncertain memory. Distant wars appeared heroic and splendid instead

of sordid and cruel to innocent people as today's war photographers show us in behind-the-scenes pictures. Similarly photographs now reveal the sufferings of people who live in bad conditions or are underpriveleged in various ways – situations which were hidden from and often ignored by governments in previous centuries.

Newspaper photographs have reported many amusing and dramatic moments over the years. One example is the picture of the nude 'streaker' shown below. Notice how all the expressions work so well in this picture – the man remonstrating, the policeman amused, the official outraged, and the crowd roaring with laughter in the background.

The actuality and realism of news pictures has made reporting come alive. Personalities in entertainment, sport, the arts, politics, and members of the royal

31.1 (Courtesy Syndication International Ltd)

138

31.2 Everyone escaped this fire. (Courtesy Popperfoto/Reuter)

31.3 (Courtesy Stephen Dalton, Natural History Photographic Agency)

family have been seen not just as stuffy portraits but as real people in close-up and at unguarded moments. Your great-grand-parents were the first to be able to record easily the appearance of their loved ones. Earlier nineteenth century families could do this only by employing an artist – something only the comparatively rich could afford. Today photographs are frozen memories of our parents when young and reminders of events such as parties and outings, probably the nearest thing we shall ever get to a 'time machine'.

Thanks to photography scenes of dramatic incidents can be shown as if you were there, transmitted to publications around the world within minutes of the event taking place. Some people argue that such pictures just feed voyeurism and idle curiosity; for others the response is heartfelt human concern. Again, actuality pictures of this kind later provide important evidence of 'how it was'. Imagine what a difficult and lengthy job it would be to describe all the details in Figure 31.2, using words alone.

31.4 War refugees (Courtesy Syndication International Ltd)

Sometimes news pictures make their point in a very simple and direct way, like Figure 31.4. Here we do not need to see the detail of faces – this tragic aftermath of children caught up in war is communicated by the shapes and composition. However, remember from your practical photographic experience how lighting, choice of background and environment can influence a subject's appearance. Similarly, situations can be implied in documentary pictures which did not in fact exist, just because two unconnected events happen to be shown in the same frame, or through someone's fleeting expression.

Photography has also given us real information which would be impossibly difficult to acquire any other way. One man can go up in an aircraft and bring back pictures such as Figure 31.5 of a fortified medieval town in the Netherlands. Historians, geographers, and archaeologists can read a great deal of information from this print without also having to fly over the town. Moreover, since a photograph can be read in any language, students in any country in the world can learn from it too. By being printed in books and periodicals the information reaches millions of people. This multi-lingual aspect of photography is of great value in teaching and explaining how to do things. For example, it can clearly show to a worker on the other side of the world how to operate a process safely and efficiently.

Photographs are very persuasive too. Advertisers use them cleverly to exaggerate and gently distort reality in favour of what they are selling. The picture may be 'hard sell' meaning it shows strongly the actual product being sold, such as the chocolates (Figure 31.7). The 'soft sell' approach uses a desirable situation and suggests that this follows from using their product (Figure 31.8). Advertisements can be very convincing because we tend to accept that a *photograph* is inherently more accurate and truthful than a *drawing*. You have to learn to be on your guard and discriminate between fact and implied fact.

Photographic materials and x-rays allow us to record the contents of visually opaque objects. The most important example of this is medical radiography, where shadow pictures of bones and internal organs help doctors to diagnose and check on the progress of treatment. But radiography is also used to learn about the internal structure of objects such as the sea shell in Figure 31.6 and for checking the soundness of metal components such as turbine blades.

The ability of photography to render fine detail means that it can be used for the production of miniaturised components. The wiring for an electronic circuit can be drawn on paper, photographed, reduced down in size and printed and etched into metal to give a printed circuit for a tiny transmitter. Photographs also

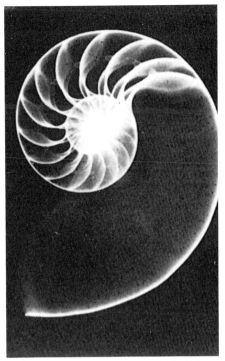

31.6 X-ray of sea shell (Courtesy Kodak Ltd)

31.5 Naarden, Netherlands

141

31.7 'Hard sell' advertisement

31.8 'Soft sell' advertisement

freeze incredibly brief events in time, or show changes over a long period. Scientists use ultra fast shutters and special lighting to record what happens when sub-atomic particles collide or an explosive is detonated. Sequences of photographs made over days and weeks can reveal the gradual growth of a plant. Time scales are thus altered to suit us, so that we can study and analyse events at leisure.

Similarly photography can observe and record for us underwater, or underground. The behaviour of animals and birds at night can be revealed, like the barn owl returning with a young rat to its nest, Figure 31.3. (This was photographed from a a hide, using flashguns left and right of the bird.) Notice how many pictures taken for scientific and technical purposes such as Figures 31.6 are not only records but visually satisfying too.

Photography proves to us the visual similarity between natural structures which are extremely big and extremely small. Figure 31.9 shows what could be a planet, but is in fact a tiny pollen grain (one of the kind that causes hay fever) shown here over two thousand times its actual size. It was photographed through an electron microscope. And what appears to be hoar frost on a leaf in Figure 31.10 is really the snow-covered tops of mountains in the Himalayas, photographed from an earth orbiting satellite more than 100 miles above. Pictures like this can be used to calculate the likely flow of water to valley areas when the winter snows melt.

So photography has enormously extended our vision, into things much too big or small, fast or slow to see by eye. It is the great *communicator*, together with its offspring film and television. It trains, sells and entertains us. Perhaps most important of all it helps to explain people – their joys and fears, poverty or pride – to others, whatever their language and wherever they live. Being able to take photographs is as powerful a means of communicating ideas and information as being able to speak or write.

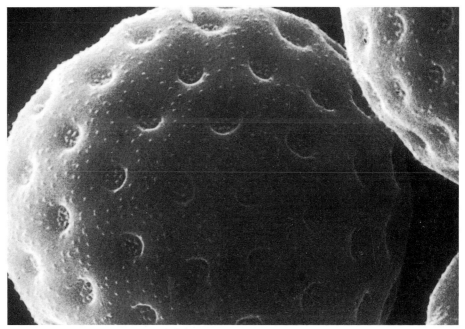

31.9 (Above) Courtesy Dr P. Echlin

31.10 Courtesy NASA

143

Appendix A – Roll and Sheet-film Cameras

The great majority of modern cameras use 35 mm film, but other cameras are made to accept larger picture format rollfilm or individual sheet films. You will also find many older, second-hand cameras needing films of this kind. Unlike 35 mm material in its light-tight cassette, rollfilm comes on an open spool attached to lightproof 'backing paper' (Figure A.2). Film and backing paper are rolled up tightly together so that light cannot reach the sensitive surface during loading. Inside the camera they wind up tightly onto an identical take-up spool after exposure, ready for unloading.

The main rollfilm still in general use is 120 size. This allows pictures 6 cm (2¼ in) wide. Some cameras give twelve pictures 6 × 6 cm to a film, others ten pictures 6 × 7 cm or sixteen 6 × 4.5 cm. Negatives this size need less enlargement than 35 mm film so you can make big prints which are relatively grain-free.

A few large format cameras use individual sheets of film, typically 4 × 5 in. Each sheet has first to be loaded into a film holder in the dark (see facing page). Using sheet film allows you to process each exposure individually; and the still larger negative gives even finer grain and detail.

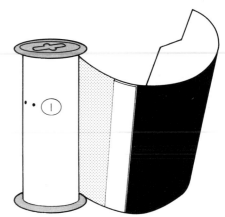

A.2 How the start of a 120 rollfilm is attached to its light-proof backing paper

Twin lens reflex cameras

Some rollfilm cameras are designed as *twin lens reflexes*. As Figure A.1 shows, the camera body has two lenses – one for viewing and focusing, the other for shooting. The upper or 'viewing' lens reflects off a fixed mirror and forms an image on a ground glass screen on top of the camera. The lower lens is the one which takes the photograph, and is fitted with a shutter and a diaphragm within the lens. To use a TLR camera you load it with a rollfilm, set shutter speed and *f*-number according to the light and then look down onto the focusing screen to see what you are photographing.

Turning the focusing knob moves *both* lenses backwards and forwards, so that when your subject is sharply imaged on the ground glass the taking lens is also correctly positioned to give a sharp image on film. Pressing the release fires the bladed shutter, exposing the picture. The image on the focusing screen does not disappear at the moment of shooting, like a single lens reflex. It is easy to shoot from low viewpoints and still see to focus. However, since viewing and taking lenses are separate, the camera suffers parallax error (page 12) especially in close-up work. It is also bulky, and few models accept inter-changeable lenses. Another disadvantage is that the picture on the focusing screen appears reversed left to right, which can be irritating when trying to follow a moving subject.

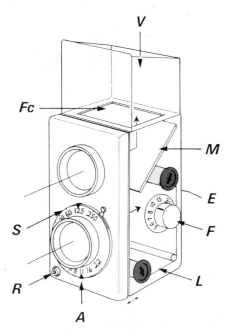

A.1 (above) Rollfilm twin lens reflex camera. Fc: Focusing screen. S: Shutterspeed control. R: Release for shutter. A: Aperture control. V: Viewfinder. M: Mirror (fixed). E: Exposure counter at back of camera. F: Focusing control. L: Light sensitive film

View cameras

These sheet film cameras, Figure A.3, look large and professional but are really simple in construction. They are designed always to be used on a tripod. The front panel carries a lens with diaphragm and shutter; the back simply has a large ground glass focusing screen. Focusing controls allow the two panels to be moved towards or away from each other along a rail, and flexible square-shaped bellows between the panels keep out the light. Other knobs

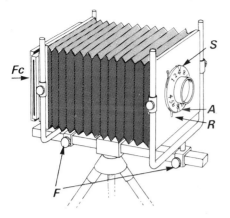

A.3 5 × 4 in. technical camera. Fc: Focusing screen. S: Shutter speed dial. A: Aperture control. R: Shutter release. F: Focus controls

allow sliding or swinging of the front and back panels. These are known as 'camera movements' and used to help control depth of field or shape distortion.

The large focusing screen is helpful for carefully composing still-life subjects in the studio. It is possible to focus very close subjects too. However, these cameras are large, slow and cumbersome to use; and you have to get used to checking an image which is upside down. The picture sequence on the right shows how the camera is used, starting in the darkroom where each sheet of film is loaded into a special holder. When the film holder is slipped into the camera it replaces the focusing screen, taking up the same position. A panel or 'darkslide' in the holder is then removed to reveal the emulsion side of the film to the (dark) inside of the camera. As soon as the exposure has been made using the shutter on the lens, the darkslide must be replaced. The holder is then withdrawn from the camera and taken to the darkroom where the film is removed and processed.

A.4 (Right) How a picture is exposed with a 4 × 5 in camera, using a sheet film holder

Appendix B – Using a Hand Meter

Most modern 35mm cameras have a light meter built into the camera to measure the subject and calculate exposure. But this feature is often lacking in older cameras, and in cameras taking larger formats (Appendix A). You can therefore buy a separate, hand-held exposure meter. Used properly this will measure your subject and read out the appropriate combination of *f*-number and shutter speed for the film you are using.

A small hand-meter simplifies the making of local readings of highlight and shadow parts as it is easier to bring near to the subject than moving the whole camera. In fact you can measure exposure without taking out the camera (an advantage for candid work), and one meter will also serve any number or types of camera. However, as a hand-meter does not measure light through the camera lens you must be prepared to adjust the exposure settings it suggests when shooting close-ups – especially if close enough to need extension tubes or bellows, see facing page.

A traditional hand-meter, Figure B.1, has a light-sensitive cell at the back to measure the light reflected from your subject. You first set the ISO rating of your film in a window on the front dial, point the meter, note the number shown under a moving needle, and set this against an arrow on the dial. Suitable combinations of lens aperture and shutter setting, all of which will result in correct exposure, then appear lined up in the lower part of the dial. You choose the one giving the depth of field or movement blur effects you need, and set the camera accordingly.

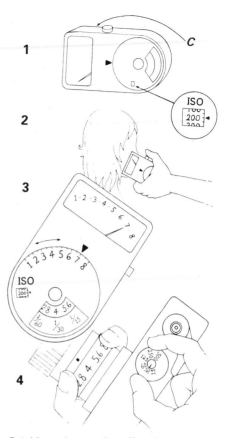

B.1 Measuring, reading off, and setting exposure

Different ways of making readings

Any hand-meter pointed generally at your subject from the camera position will give an exposure reading based on the assumption that the subject has roughly equal areas of light and dark. This is like a general reading made by an in-camera meter. Some hand-meters have a white plastic diffuser which slides over the cell. You then hold the meter at the subject, its cell facing the camera, when taking your reading. This 'incident light' single measurement scrambles all the light reaching parts of the subject seen by the camera, ignoring light or dark unimportant background.

For still greater accuracy take *two* reflected light readings, one from the darkest important shadowed area, the other from the brightest important highlight area. Then split the difference between the two. For example, in Figure B.2, readings were taken about six inches from the lightest (6) and then the darkest (3) parts of the man's head. The dial was set to the midway position – in this case 4½ – to find correct camera settings.

When a subject cannot be approached so closely try taking readings from nearby substitutes under the same lighting. For example, in Figure B.3 the photographer is reading off the matching skin of his or her own hands – first turned towards, then away from the same lighting received by the face. Again, in landscapes you can read off the grass at your feet for grass on a distant hill – provided both are under the same lighting conditions. Remember, when taking any form of reading not to accidentally measure the shadow of either you or the meter. If the lighting is so poor that the meter fails to give a reading at all, try measuring off a white card, or shirt, etc., and then expose for *six times* as long as it suggests.

Be particularly careful when a great deal of light is coming from behind your main subject – perhaps from a sky background, as in the picture on page 71. Here it is essential to limit your reading to the face since a general reading will register much too much sky light and the face will be underexposed.

Exposure increase for close-ups

When you are shooting subjects very close-up (using extension rings or bellows to get a sharp image), the image is less bright then with distant subjects – even though lighting and *f*-number remain the same. Inside the camera the effect is like being in a darkened room with a slide projector being moved away from the screen (the film). As you focus the camera lens for an ever-closer subject the image becomes bigger but also *dimmer*.

If your camera measures exposure through the lens itself this change is taken into account by the metering system; but when using any other form of meter you must increase the exposure shown to take this loss of light into account. In practice exposure only starts to become significantly affected when your subject is closer than about five times the focal length of the lens you are using, e.g. subjects closer than 250 mm from a 50 mm lens. The increase needed soon becomes quite high as you work closer still:

For a subject this close to a 50 mm lens:	Increase exposure shown on the meter by:
21 cm	1½ times
17	2
10	4
9	5

Increase the exposure either by giving a slower shutter speed, *or* by opening up the lens aperture – one *f*-number for a × 2 increase, one and a half for × 3, and so on.

You can also calculate exposure increase as follows:

Multiply the exposure shown on the meter by $(M + 1)^2$

where M = Height of image divided by height of subject.

Example: You are photographing a 30 mm high postage stamp so that it appears 15 mm high on the film. Magnification is therefore 0.5, and you must multiply exposure by 1.5^2 which is 2.25 (i.e. open up the lens aperture by just over one *f*-number).

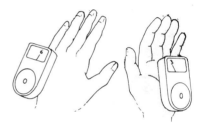

B2–3 Making highlight and shadow readings. Top: direct from subject itself. Bottom: from substitute hands in direct light and shadow. (Meter calculator was then set midway between 3 and 6)

147

Appendix C – Chemically Treating Black and White Prints

Even after you have made a black and white print, there are still several ways you can alter the image by chemical means. You can decide to make your picture lighter in tone; or bleach away parts to white paper; or tone it so that the neutral black image turns into a colour. All these chemical treatments are carried out in trays, working under ordinary room lighting.

Start off with a fully fixed and washed print. If it has already dried re-soak it in water for 2–3 minutes, then blot it or wipe off surplus liquid. Working on a damp print helps to allow the chemicals to act evenly.

Reducing (lightening) the image

Farmer's reducer is a mixture of potassium ferricyanide and hypo (see formula, facing page). This forms a yellow solution which you apply on a cottonwool swab to overdark parts of the picture. Then immediately hold your print under a cold water tap to halt the reduction. Examine the effect carefully. You repeat the process – just a little at a time – until the part of the print (or the entire image) is sufficiently lightened. If you go too far there is no way you can bring back the image again. Finally re-fix and wash the whole print.

Farmer's reducer has its most rapid effect on the palest tones in an image, so it is excellent for the overall 'brightening up' of pictures with veiled over (grey) highlights. Don't expect to rescue a really dark print this way however – if overdone the reducer leaves a yellowish stain and brownish black tones. Farmer's reducer can also be used to lighten very dense, low contrast negatives; i.e. overexposed and underdeveloped. At the same time it greatly exaggerates the graininess of the image.

Bleaching

By using an iodine bleacher you can erase chosen parts of your print right down to white paper, without leaving any final stain. It is ideal for removing an unwanted background to a subject, leaving it with a 'cutout' appearance. Two separate solutions are needed – the bleacher itself, and a tray of print-strength fixer.

As Figure C.1 shows, paint over the unwanted area of your print with a swab of cottonwool (changing to a water-colour brush when working close to the edges of fine detail). A strong brown stain immediately appears, with the black image fast vanishing beneath it. Wait until the unwanted parts have lost all their black silver, then rinse the whole print in water for at least 30 seconds. Next put it in the fixer solution for 5 minutes or so until the brown stain has completely disappeared, leaving clean white paper. Finally, wash the print for the same time recommended for your printing paper after regular fixing.

Sepia toning

Changing the print image from black into sepia is the simplest and most popular toning process. It gives a rich sepia or chocolate colour, like a 19th century photograph. Sepia toning is also advisable before hand tinting (see page 96).

You need two separate solutions, bleacher and toner. Slide the print into the tray of bleacher, face up, and rock it for a minute or so until the once black image is bleached to a pale straw colour. You then rinse it under the cold water tap and place it in a tray of toner solution. The picture reappears in a sepia colour within a few seconds, but needs 2–3 minutes

C.1 Erasing the background from a print with iodine bleach

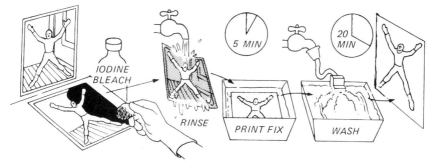

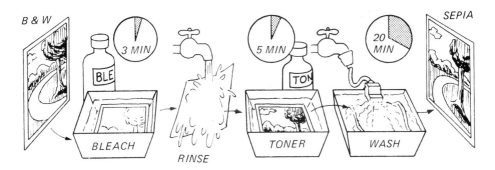

C.2 Routine for sepia toning prints

to reach full richness and depth. You finish off by washing and drying in exactly the same way as when making the print in the first instance.

The image now consists of brownish silver sulphide instead of the usual black metallic silver. This is very permanent – you cannot return a sepia print to black. Remember too that with toners of this kind bleaching is essential before the black image can become sepia. You can therefore *selectively* bleach, say, just the background to your main subject by applying bleacher on a swab. Only this area then becomes sepia in the toner, leaving the main image black.

Another alternative is to dilute the bleacher with an equal volume of water to slow its action. You then immerse the whole print but remove it before darkest greys and shadows have lost their black appearance. After completing the toning stage of the process as normal your picture consists of a mixture of sepia and black. Results have richer brown-black tones than full toning. And if you don't like the result just re-bleach your print to affect the remaining black parts and tone the print again to get a fully sepia image.

You can also buy kits of multitoner chemicals, typically consisting of a bleacher and a range of toners each of which will result in a different colour image. A kit with yellow, magenta and blue toners permits you to mix them in varying proportions (blue and yellow to get green, for example) and so form a wide choice of image hues. Most results are rather garish; some are not very permanent and change with time.

Chemicals required

Farmer's reducer and most toners can be bought as packs of ready-weighed powders and liquids from manufacturers such as Tetenal. This is the most convenient and, in the long run, cheapest way of working. To make up your own solutions, however, prepare them from the following chemicals. Follow the handling precautions described on page 150.

Iodine Bleacher

Warm water	400 ml
Potassium iodide	8 g
Iodine	2 g
Water up to	500 ml

Farmer's Reducer

(A) Potassium Ferricyanide	5 g
Water	500 ml
(B) Sodium Thiosulphate (hypo crystals)	80 g
Warm water	500 ml

Mix equal quantities of A and B just before use (does not keep as a single solution).

Sepia toning

Bleach in	
Potassium Ferricyanide	20 g
Potassium Bromide	20 g
Water up to	1 litre
Tone in	
Sodium Sulphide	20 g
Water up to	1 litre

The sulphide in this formula gives off a 'bad eggs' smell, especially when diluted. Use in a well-ventilated area, away from films and papers.

Appendix D – Health and Safety in Photography

The equipment and processes used in photography are not particularly hazardous, provided you take one or two (mostly common sense) precautions. For example, the use of electrical equipment in the studio, or within the darkroom in the presence of water and dim lighting clearly requires care. Similarly when you are using photographic chemicals it is best to adopt working habits which pay due regard to your health.

Electrical equipment

Remember that studio spotlights and floodlights produce heat as well as light. The *bottom* of the lamphead is always cooler than the *top*, so only grip the bottom when tilting the light. Never drape any diffusing or filtering material you may be using over a lamphead. Instead arrange to support it a foot or so in front of the lamp (even just hold it there when you take the picture). Keep lamps and curtains well apart for similar reasons, and don't leave your lamps on in an empty room.

Each lighting unit needs a plug fitted with an appropriate fuse. Lamp wattage divided by the supply voltage tells how many amperes are drawn. Fit a fuse rated just slightly above this figure, e.g. a 5 amp fuse if the lamp draws four or less amps. Just fitting a 15 amp fuse in every plug reduces your protection. All lighting equipment should be earthed ('grounded') through a third wire.

Watch out, with items like lamps which you move about, that cable does not fray where it enters the lamphead, and that the connections at each end have not worked loose. Never try to remove a bulb from its socket whilst it is still hot, and make sure your lighting unit is disconnected before fitting a new lamp. Be careful too not to have the power cable stretched between socket and lamphead so that you can trip over it, or have the unit set up in a way that makes it unstable and top-heavy.

Most flashguns have two circuits – a trigger circuit to the shutter which uses a very low and harmless current, and an internal higher-powered circuit to the flash tube. So never try opening up the internal electrics to repair your unit. Even though battery operated it may be storing enough electricity to give you a powerful shock.

In the darkroom, with water present, it is even more important to have your electrical equipment – enlarger, safelight, ventilator – properly fused and earthed (see page 115). Avoid having sockets or switches where someone might grasp them with a wet hand – near the sink, for example. If possible have all switches fitted to the ceiling and operated by non-conductive pull-cords. Avoid running wiring under or close to sinks, metal drying cabinets, etc. Power supply outlets should be at benchtop height, never at floor level in case of flooding.

Care with chemicals

Handle photographic chemicals with the same care as other chemicals used around the home. Always read any warning on the label, especially if what you are about to use is unfamiliar. If any contents are hazardous the container will have first aid measures labelled too.

Avoid splashing chemicals into your eyes or onto your skin, particularly skin that is dry and chapped. A few people may have an adverse reaction to chemicals such as developers, resulting in skin irritation. Waterproof gloves are then essential when film processing or printing. It is always a good idea anyway to wear simple eye protectors and gloves (rubber or plastic) when preparing chemicals, especially if you are dissolving chemicals in powdered form. Never use a punctured glove, though – it can give your hand prolonged contact with trapped liquid chemical.

Wearing gloves can be uncomfortable and impractical if you are working for long sessions constantly moving from wet to dry bench operations, as in printing. At least then keep your hands out of solutions by using tongs or paddles to move chemical-covered prints.

Always try to mix chemicals where the ventilation is good and there is running water nearby to dilute any splashes. If you spill any chemical clean it up as soon as possible. Spilt solution soon evaporates, leaving a chemical dust that blows about. This is easily inhaled or accumulates in odd corners of your darkroom.

Don't have food or drink in any room where chemicals are used. Make sure all your storage containers are accurately labelled, and *never store chemicals in food or drink containers*. Someone else may assume they are for consumption. For similar reasons keep all photographic chemicals out of the reach of children. Don't store chemicals, or solutions, in a refrigerator or freezer.

Glossary of photographic terms

AE lock (AE-L) Locks an *automatic exposure* setting in the camera's memory.

AF lock (AF-L) Locks an *autofocus* lens in its present focus setting.

Angle of View The extent of the view taken in by the lens. It varies with focal length for any particular format size. The angle made at the lens across the image diagonal.

Aperture (of lens) Size of the lens opening through which light passes. The relative aperture is calibrated in *f*-numbers, being the diameter of the beam of incident light on and allowed to pass through the lens, divided into its focal length. Widest relative apertures therefore have lowest *f*-numbers. All lenses set to the same *f*-number give images of a (distant) scene at equal brightness.

Aperture preview Button on some SLR cameras to close the lens to the *aperture* set for photography. Allows you to visually check *depth of field* in the viewfinder.

Autofocus (AF) System by which the lens automatically focuses the image of a selected part of your subject.

Av Aperture value. *AE camera* metering mode by which you choose aperture, and the metering system sets shutter speed. (Also called aperture priority.)

ASA Stands for (obsolete) American Standards Association. The initials were once used for a film speed rating system. Now replaced by ISO.

'B' Setting Brief or Bulb. On this setting the camera shutter stays open for as long as the release button remains depressed.

Bracketing (exposure) Taking several pictures of your subject at different exposure times or aperture settings. E.g. half and double as well as the estimated correct exposure.

Bromide Paper Light-sensitive photographic paper for enlarging or contact printing. Carries a predominantly silver bromide emulsion. Must be handled in appropriate (usually amber or orange) safelighting.

Burning-in Giving additional exposure time to one area of an enlargement in order to make the picture darker in tone.

Camera Obscura A dark chamber to which light is admitted through a small hole, producing an inverted image of the scene outside, opposite the hole.

Cassette Light-tight container for 35mm camera film. See page 17.

CD-ROM Compact disc with read-only memory.

Close-ups Photographs in which the picture area is filled with a relatively small part of the subject (e.g. a single head). Usually photographed from close to the subject but may be shot from further away using a long focus lens.

Close-up attachments Accessories which enable the camera to focus subjects which are closer than the nearest distance the lens normally allows.

Contact printing Printing with light, the object (typically a negative) being in direct contact with the light sensitive material.

Colour balance A colour photograph which closely resembles the original subject appearance is said to have 'correct' colour balance. Mis-matching film and lighting (wrong colour temperature) gives a cast which shows up mostly in grey tones and pale tints.

Colour temperature A means of describing the colour content of a 'white' light source. Based on the temperature (Absolute scale, expressed in kelvins) to which a black metallic body would have to be heated to match the light. E.g. Household lamp 2800 K, Photoflood 3400 K.

Complementary colours Opposite or 'negative' colours to the primary colours of light (Blue, Green and Red). Each is made up from the full spectrum less the primary colour, e.g. the complementary of Red is Blue plus Green = Cyan. Similarly Magenta is complementary to Green and Yellow to Blue.

Conjugate distances Optical term for the associated positions of object and image in relation to a lens.

Contrast The difference (ratio) between the darkest and brightest parts. In a scene this depends on lighting, and the reflecting properties of objects. In a photograph there is also the effect of exposure level, degree of development, printing paper, etc.

Cropping Cutting out unwanted (edge) parts of a picture, typically at the printing or mounting stage.

Daylight colour film Colour film balanced for use with flash, daylight, or daylight-matching strip tubes (5500 K).

DIN Stands for Deutche Industrie Norm (German Industrial Standard). DIN numbers denoted a film's relative sensitivity to light. Halving or doubling speed is shown by decrease or increase of the DIN number by *three*. Now incorporated in ISO and given degree symbol.

Depth of field Distance between nearest and farthest parts of the subject sharply imaged at the same time. Greatest with small lens apertures (high *f*-numbers) distant scenes, and shortest focal length lenses.

Developer Chemicals, normally in solution, able to convert the invisible (latent) image on exposed photographic material into visible form. Converts (reduces) the light-struck silver halide grains to black metallic silver.

Developing agents Chemicals (typically Phenidone, Metol and hydroquinone) able to change light-struck silver halides into black metallic silver.

Diffuse lighting Scattered illumination, the visual result is gentle modelling of the subject with mild or non-existent shadows.

Dodging Local shading in enlarging, usually by means of a piece of opaque material on a thin wire.

DX coding Coding printed onto film cassette denoting speed, length, etc. Read by sensors in the film compartment of most 35mm cameras.

Emulsion Suspension of minute silver halide crystals in gelatine which, coated on film or paper, forms the light sensitive material used in photography.

Enlarger Optical projector to give enlarged (or reduced) images which can then be exposed on to light sensitive paper or film. See page 120.

Enlarging easel (masking frame) Flat board with adjustable flaps used on the enlarger baseboard to hold paper flat during exposure.

Expiry date Develop-before date, stamped on film boxes.

Exposed A light sensitive material which has received exposure to an image. Usually relates to the stage after exposure and before processing.

Exposure Submitting photographic material to the action of light, usually by means of a camera or enlarger.

Exposure latitude The amount by which a photographic emulsion may be under- or overexposed, yet still give an acceptable image when processed.

Exposure meter Instrument which measures light intensities falling on, or reflected off the subject, and indicates corresponding camera settings (shutter and aperture). See page 146.

Extension tubes Rings or short tubes mounted between camera body and lens to space the lens further away from the film and so allow the sharp focusing of very close subjects.

ƒ-numbers See **Aperture**.

Fill-in Illumination to lighten shadows, reducing contrast.

Film speed Measure of sensitivity of film to light. Usually expressed as an ISO figure.

Filter, lens Sheet of (usually dyed) gelatine or glass. Used over the camera lens mainly to reduce the light (neutral density grey filter) or to absorb particular wavelengths from the light beam.

Fixer Chemical (basically a solution of sodium thiosulphate plus potassium metabisulphite as acidifier). Used after development to make soluble those parts of a photographic image unaffected by the developer. Photographs can thereafter be handled in normal lighting.

Fixed focus Camera lens set for a fixed subject distance. Non-adjustable.

Fixing agent Chemical (usually sodium thiosulphate) able to change silver halides into colourless soluble salts.

Flare Scattered light which dilutes the image, lowering contrast and seeming to reduce sharpness. Mostly occurs when the subject is back-lit.

Flash contacts Electrical contacts, normally within the mechanism of the camera shutter, which come together at the appropriate moment to trigger the flash unit. Older shutters may be fitted with X and M contact sockets. Use X for electronic flash.

Flash (Electronic) Equipment which gives a brief, brilliant flash of light by discharging an electronic capacitor through a small gas-filled tube.

Given time to recharge, a unit gives many thousands of flashes, usually triggered by contacts within the camera shutter.

Flash factor see **Guide Number**.

'Flat' images Images which are low in tonal contrast, appearing grey and muddy.

Floodlamp Studio lighting units consisting of a large reflector containing a photolamp or other pearl glass lamp. Gives diffuse lighting.

Focal length In a simple lens the distance (in millimetres) between lens and position of a sharp image for a subject a great distance away. (In complex designs such as telephoto, measured from the rear nodal point). A 'normal' lens has a focal length approximately equivalent to the *diagonal* of the picture format it covers. i.e. 50 mm for 36×24 mm.

Focal plane The plane – normally flat and at right-angles to the lens axis – on which a sharp image is formed. In the camera the emulsion surface of the film must be in the focal plane at the moment of exposure to record a focused image.

Focus priority (trap focus) *Autofocus* camera mode by which you cannot release the shutter until the lens has sharply focused your subject.

Focusing Changing the lens-to-image (or lens-to-subject) distance, until a sharp image is formed.

Fog Allowing random light to reach light-sensitive material, as in opening the camera back accidentally or leaving a packet of paper open. Also caused by bad storage or contaminated or over-prolonged development (chemical fog).

Form Three-dimensionality. Height, breadth and depth.

Format Height and breadth dimensions of the picture area.

Glossy paper Photographic paper which can give prints with a shiny, glossy surface.

Grade, of paper Classification of black and white photographic papers by the gradation they offer between black and white. Soft (Grade 1) paper gives a wider range of grey tones than Hard (Grade 3). See also Variable contrast paper.

Grain Irregularly shaped, microscopically small clumps of black silver making up the processed photographic image. Detectable on enlargement, particularly if the film was fast (say, ISO 1000 or over) and overdeveloped. Hard paper also emphasises film grain.

Guide number (flash factor) Figure denoting the relative power of a flash source. The GN is the light-to-subject distance (usually in metres) multiplied by the ƒ-number for correct exposure. E.g. GN of 16 = 2 m at ƒ8 or 1 m at ƒ16. (Unless *film speed* is quoted, factor refers to ISO 100 film).

'Hard' images Images with harsh tonal contrasts – mostly blacks and whites with few intermediate grey tones.

'Hard' light sources Harsh source of illumination, giving strong clear-cut shadows. Tends to dramatise form and texture.

Hyperfocal distance Nearest subject rendered sharp when the lens is focused for infinity. Focused for the hyperfocal distance and without change of *f*-number, depth of field extends from half this distance to infinity.

Hypo Abbreviation of hyposulphate of soda, an incorrect early name for sodium thiosulphate. Popular name for fixing bath.

Incident light attachment Diffusing disc or dome (usually of white plastic) placed over the cell of a hand-held exposure meter to make readings *towards the light source*. Calculator dial is then used in normal way. Gives results similar to reading off an average subject or grey card.

Infinity A distance so great that light from a given point reaches the camera as virtually parallel rays. In practice, distances of about 1000 times the focal length or over. Written on lens focusing mounts as 'inf' or a symbol like an 8 on its side.

Inverse square law 'When a surface is illuminated by a point source of light the intensity of light at the surface is inversely proportional to the square of its distance from the source.' In other words if you double the lamp distance light spreads over a larger area and illumination drops to $\frac{1}{2} \times \frac{1}{2} = \frac{1}{4}$ of its previous value. Forms the basis of flash Guide Numbers and close-up exposure increases. Does not apply to large diffuse sources or the (extremely distant) sun.

ISO International Standards Organization. In the ISO film speed system halving or doubling of speed is denoted by halving or doubling number. Also often incorporates *DIN* figure, e.g. ISO 400/27° film is twice as sensitive as ISO 200/24°.

K (Kelvins) Measurement unit of lighting and *colour temperature*.

Large format (cameras) Normally refers to cameras taking negatives larger than 120 rollfilm size.

Latent image The invisible image contained by the photographic material after exposure but before development. Stored protected from light, damp and chemical fumes a latent image can persist for years.

Long focal length lens Lens with focal length longer than considered 'normal' for picture format. Gives larger detail, narrower angle of view. Almost all such lenses are *telephoto* types.

Macro lens Lens intended for close-up photography, able to focus well forward from its infinity position for subjects a few inches away, gives highest quality image at such distances.

Macrophotography Photography at very close subject range.

Masking frame See *Enlarging easel*.

Monochrome image Single coloured. Usually implies black image, but also applies to one which is toned. i.e. sepia.

Montage An image constructed by combining what were originally several separate images. Figure 23.4 is an example.

Negative image Image in which blacks, whites and tones are reversed, relative to the original subject. Colour negatives have the colours represented by their *complementaries*.

'Normal' lens The lens regarded as standard for the picture format. i.e. having a *focal length* approximately equal to its diagonal.

Overdevelopment Giving too long, or too much agitation in the developer, or having too high a temperature, or developer too concentrated. This results in excessive density, and exaggerated grain structure in the developed material.

Overexposure Exposing photographic material to too much light because the image is too bright, or exposure time too long. Results in excessive density in the final image.

Panning Rotating or swinging the camera about a vertical axis.

Panchromatic Photographic materials sensitive to all visible colours, recording them in various shades of grey. Should be processed in total darkness or an exceedingly dark safelight. All general purpose films are of this kind.

Parallax error Viewpoint difference between the picture seen in the viewfinder and as seen by the camera lens. See page 12.

Photographic lamps Generalised term now often applied to both 3200 K studio lamps (floods and spots) and the brighter, short life 3400 K photoflood lamps.

Photomicrography Photography through a microscope.

Positive image One in which blacks, whites and tones approximate those of the original subject; or colours are reproduced normally.

Preservative (developer) Chemical (typically sodium sulphite) included in a developer to help preserve developing agents from oxidation.

Printing in See **Burning in**.

'Pushing' Slang term for uprating film speed.

Rapid fixer Fixing bath using ammonium thiosulphate or thiocyanate instead of the normal sodium thiosulphate. Enables fixing time to be greatly reduced, but is more expensive.

Reciprocity law failure Normally the effect of dim light, or small lens aperture, can be counteracted by giving a long exposure time. But this reciprocal relationship (half the brightness = double the exposure time) increasingly breaks down with exposure times beyond one second. The film then behaves as if having a lower speed rating. Colour films may also show incorrect colour balance.

'Red eye' The iris of each eye in portraits shows red instead of black. Caused by using flash directed from close to the lens.

Reflex camera Camera with viewfinder system using a mirror and focusing screen.

Refraction Change of direction of a ray of light passing obliquely from one transparent medium into another of different density e.g. from air into glass. The basic reason why lenses bend light rays and so form images.

Resin coated (RC) bromide paper Bromide paper having a water-repellent plastic base. As chemicals are not absorbed by the base material RC papers require less washing, dry more rapidly and generally processes faster than fibre base papers.

Reversal film Film which can be processed to

give a positive image direct. Colour slide films are of this type. Several normal black and white films can be reversal processed.

Rollfilm Photographic film, usually 6.2 mm wide (known as 120 or 220) attached to numbered backing paper and rolled on a flanged spool.

Safelight Darkroom light source filtered to illuminate only in a colour to which photographic material is insensitive. The correct colour varies with type of emulsion, e.g. orange for bromide papers.

Selective focusing Using a shallow depth of field (i.e. by means of a wide lens aperture) and focusing so that only one selected zone of the subject is sharply recorded. A method of separating out and giving emphasis to one element of a scene.

Shading, or dodging, in printing Preventing the image light from acting on a selected area of the picture for a time during the exposure, causing this part to be *lighter* in the final print.

Sheet film Film supplied as individual sheets, usually 10 or 25 to a box.

Shutter Mechanical device to control the time the light is allowed to act on the film. Usually consists of metal blades within the lens, or two blinds passing one after another just in front of the film, the exposure occurring in the gap between them (focal plane shutter).

Silver halides Light sensitive compounds of silver with the halogens (iodine, bromine, etc.). Normally white or creamy yellow in colour. Used as the main sensitive constituent of photographic emulsions.

Single lens reflex (SLR) . Camera in which the viewfinder image is formed by the picture-taking lens. See page 14.

Soft focus Image in which outlines are slightly spread or diffused.

'Soft' light sources See **Diffuse lighting.**

'Spotlight' A compact filament lamp, reflector and lens forming one lighting unit. Gives hard direct illumination, variable from narrow to broad beam.

Still video Original general term for cameras recording still pictures by electronic rather than chemical (film) means.

Stop-bath Stage in processing which arrests the action of the previous solution (e.g. a weak solution of acetic acid used between development and fixation).

'T' setting Setting found on some large format camera shutters for time exposures. Pressing the release opens the shutter, which then remains open until pressed for a second time.

Telephoto lens Long focus lens of compact design (lens is physically closer to the film than its focal length).

Test strip One of a series of test exposures on a piece of printing paper, then processed to see which gives the most satisfactory result.

Texture Surface qualities such as roughness, smoothness, hairiness, etc.

Through-the-lens (TTL) metering Measuring exposure by a meter built into the camera body, which measures the intensity of light passing through the picture-taking lens.

Time exposure General term for a long duration exposure.

Tones, tone values Areas of uniform density in a positive or negative image which can be distinguished from darker or lighter parts.

Translucent Transmitting but also diffusing light, e.g. tracing paper.

Transparency Positive image on film.

Tungsten lamps Lamps which generate light when electric current is passed through a fine tungsten wire. Household lamps, photofloods, studio lamps, etc., are all of this type.

Tungsten light film (also 'Type B' or 'Artificial light'). Colour film balanced for use with 3200 K studio lighting.

Tv. Time value. *AE camera* metering mode by which you choose shutter speed and the metering system sets aperture. (Also called shutter priority.)

Twin lens reflex Camera design using two linked lenses – one forming an image onto film, the other giving an image on a focusing screen. See page 144.

Type B colour film See **Tungsten light film.**

Uprating Shooting film at more than the manufacturer's suggested speed rating, e.g. exposing 400 ISO film as if 800 ISO. The film is then given extra development. There is a distinct limit to the degree of uprating possible before image quality suffers, i.e. development cannot fully compensate for underexposure.

Underdevelopment Giving too short a developing time; using too low a temperature, too great a dilution or old or exhausted solutions. This results in insufficient density being built up.

Underexposure Exposing photographic material to too little light, because the image is too dim or exposure time too short. Results in insufficient density and shadow detail in the final image.

Variable contrast (multigrade) paper Black and white printing paper which changes its contrast characteristics with the colour of the exposing light. Controlled by enlarger filters ranging from yellow to purple.

Viewpoint The position from which camera, and photographer, view the subject.

Wetting agent Chemical (e.g. weak detergent) which reduces the surface tension of water. Facilitates even action of developer or final wash water.

Wide angle lens Lens with a focal length much shorter than the diagonal of the format for which it is designed to be used. Gives a wide angle of view and considerable depth of field.

Zoom lens A lens which offers variation of focal length (without altering focus setting).

How they were taken

Additional technical information on pictures used in this book. Unless otherwise stated, all photographs were exposed on 400 ISO black & white, 64 ISO colour slide, or 100 ISO colour negative 35 mm film.

P.6 Simple lens (a condenser from an enlarger) forming the image of the girl outside in the garden. A white reflector was behind the hand holding film. ½ second at *f* 16. SLR.

P.8 Figs 1.7–9. Left hand picture, 5 seconds with pinhole; Centre, 1/250 second using plastic lens from cracker; Right, 1/125 second at *f* 8 with normal camera lens.

P.18 Fig 3.3. 125 ISO film, overdeveloped to give 3000 ISO. Taken in a room lit by one distant fluorescent tube, 1/250 second at *f* 2.8. Note how grain is always most apparent in the grey tones of the image – it becomes hidden in pure black or white areas.

P.19 Fig 3.4. Light source a large (rear) window plus large white reflector boards either side of the camera. 1 second at *f* 22, 32 ISO film.

P.20 Fig 4.1. ⅛ second at *f* 11.

P.21 Fig 4.2. 1/250 second at *f* 8.

P.23 Fig 4.6. Mostly backlit by one spotlight. Black paper background. Exposure measured by averaging highlight and shadow zones of bag. 5 seconds at *f* 22 for each picture.

P.23 Fig 4.7. Panned camera, 1/60 second at *f* 16. ISO 125 film.

P.25 Fig 5.4 was taken using the depth of field scale for this lens. By focusing for 4 metres depth of field extended from 1.5 metres to infinity.

P.26 Fig 5.6. Meter readings from boys' faces. Overcast weather. 1/500 second at *f* 4.

P.30 Fig 6.9. Exposure measured for the average of nearest light and dark buildings. 1/125 second at *f* 11.

P.31 Fig 6.11. 2¼ in square TLR at ground level. 1/60 second at *f* 11, being the average of one close-up reading off the wheelbarrow's side and another from the sunlit side of the dog's face. The low angle avoided a complicated background.

P.32 Fig 6.12. Exposure measured close-up from shadow only. 1/125 second at *f* 8. Printed light on very hard grade paper. 2¼ in square TLR.

P.32 Fig 6.13. Foggy winter's day. One exposure reading measured off sky (avoiding sun) directly overhead. Sun patch shaded during enlarging to make it appear stronger. 1/60 second at *f* 11.

P.34 Fig 7.3. 1/60 second at *f* 8.

P.34 Fig 7.4. A 135 mm focal length lens fills the picture with this stone detail on a Scottish castle, high above eye level. 1/125 second at *f* 5.6.

P.35 Fig 7.5. This fisheye lens fits on a Nikon single lens reflex camera body. The man in the picture held the camera about 5 cm from his open mouth. The wall behind him was one straight line. Note the immense depth of field. 1/125 second at *f* 11.

P.35 Fig 7.6. Small room, existing daylight from window, plus ceiling light. Average of readings off dark (low) and light parts of wall. 1/30 second at *f* 5.6, camera supported on stool.

P.36–7 Fig 7.8. Sleeping figure was just over one metre from the camera, background group ten metres. In Figure 7.9 nearest figures were about 25 metres, furthest figures 35 metres.

P.37 Fig 7.10. It is very difficult to predict the exact effect zooming will give. (In an SLR camera you cannot even see the image during exposure). So take several pictures at ¼ or ⅛ second settings. Use slow film, e.g. 32 ISO here.

P.39 Fig 8.3. Taken with centre-frame auto-focusing compact camera, with flash built-in close to lens.

P.39 Fig 8.4. Flashgun, mounted on camera and used direct. Unlike Fig 8.3, however, flash is 3–4 inches to one side and above lens. And a small piece of tracing paper diffuser covered the flash but not the sensor.

P.42 Fig 8.9. Automatic camera with built-in flash (diffused with tracing paper) set to 'fill-flash' mode.

P.42 Fig 8.10, 1/30 second at *f* 4. Fig 8.11, 1/60 second at *f* 5.6.

P.43 Fig 8.12. Flashgun tilted to bounce off (cream) ceiling. Resulting warm skin tones acceptable here, but beware most coloured walls/ceiling.

P.43 Fig 8.13. Flashgun mounted on camera, but reflected off white bathroom ceiling. Auto (TTL) exposure setting.

P.45 Figs 9.1–2. Christchurch harbour at dusk. Camera was almost faced into the sun, making a lens hood essential. One general light-reading taken off the sea towards the right, avoiding direct rays from the sun. 1/250 second at *f* 11. 2¼ in square TLR.

P.46 Fig 9.4. With backlighting like this it is essential to use a lens hood or at least shade the camera lens with your free hand. Otherwise scattered light may flare into the dark areas, turning them grey. 1/250 second at *f* 8.

P.47 Fig 9.5. Exposure readings averaged from face and sunlit chest.

P.50 Fig 10.1. Exposure was based on a general, overall meter reading – highlights and shadows being about equal in area. 1/125 second at *f* 8.

P.51 Fig 10.4. Existing (back) lighting, some fill-in from white wall behind camera. Exposure read for shadowed skin tones.

P.51 Fig 10.5. Required careful choice of (midway) focus and depth of field checking to ensure signboard and house recorded sharply. 1/60 second at *f* 16.

P.52 Fig 10.6. Overcast. Average of one reading off the bushes, one reading off the hand (for cat). 1/125 second at *f* 16.

P.53 Fig 10.8. Photographed almost straight into the sun, waiting until it was partly obscured by cloud. Distant fields were totally in shadow. No filter, but sky darkened in printing. One reading straight down off straw at feet. 1/125 second at *f* 22.

P.55 Fig 11.2. 2¼ in square camera, 1/10 second at

f22. Exposure was measured by a close-up reading from the water alone.

P.56 Fig 11.3. One general exposure reading taken of the window (1/500 second at f16) resulting in the shadows being underexposed. Printed light on hard grade.

P.56 Fig 11.4. Overcast day at zoo. Overall reading of animal's hide. 1/125 second at f11. Printed on hard grade paper.

P.56 Fig 11.5. Photographed through shop window quickly guessing exposure and focusing distance.

P.56 Fig 11.6. Single overall exposure reading, 1/125 second at f11. Printed on hard grade.

P.57 Fig 11.7. Objects laid out on thick white plastic, lit from beneath. Printed on very hard grade. 5×4 in camera.

P.57 Fig 11.8 A candid shot, guessing at distance and exposure. (1/250 second at f11).

P.58 Fig 12.2. Exposure measured off sunlit grass alone.

P.59 Fig 12.3. Exposure 1 second at f2.

P.60 Fig 13.1. Brilliant sunlight, some being reflected back from a concrete yard below. One overall meter reading 1/250 second at f11, old $2\frac{1}{4}$ in square camera 125 ISO film.

P.61 Fig 13.2. Photographed directly against the setting sun, using lens hood. Meter reading off a sunlit patch of beach at feet. 1/250 second at f16. Printed dark and contrasty.

P.63 Fig 14.3. Picture was cropped at top to remove a distracting skyline above hedge.

P.64 Fig 14.5. Diffused daylight from a large window plus a reflector board on the shadow side. Like 14.7 reflector helps to record some eye detail and face shape on the side furthest from the light. (Overall frontal lighting would do this too, but lose subject form and skin texture.) Highlight and shadow readings.

P.64 Fig 14.6. Wide angle lens. Lit by diffused daylight from a large window behind the camera. $\frac{1}{4}$ second at f11.

P.65 Fig 14.7. Shot with a TLR $2\frac{1}{4}$ in square camera at floor level, 1/60 second at f4. Other details see text.

P.66 Figure 15.1. Photographed from the other side of the road – the tower block being about 250 metres further away than the wall.

P.66 Fig 15.2. Back lighting also contributes to the feeling of depth here. Picture was taken from under an arch, which effectively shaded the lens. 1/250 second at f16.

P.67 Fig 15.3. One general reading off building, 1/125 second at f16. Photographed from well down the road to lessen converging vertical lines.

P.68 Fig 15.5. With colours and patterns as varied as these doors try to standardise all other factors and conditions. Here the lighting is consistently soft overcast daylight, and the camera viewpoint remains about the same height and distance from each door. Several of these pictures were taken hundreds of miles apart.

P.69 Fig 15.7. Hard, raking sunlight was essential to reveal brick texture. A few moments later the sun had moved on, and the wall was in flat shadow.

P.69 Fig 15.8. Photographed late afternoon, from the first platform of the Eiffel Tower. General exposure reading.

P.70 Fig 16.1. Situation seen at downstairs cottage window. One general reading 1/125 second at f11.

P.70 Fig 16.2. Cat peering nervously through reeded glass front door, noticed when walking along the street. Guessed exposure 1/125 second at f11. Cat vanished into the house when it heard the shutter.

P.71 Fig 16.3. Close-up meter readings from girl's face and pullover. Overcast daylight 1/60 second at f11, $2\frac{1}{4}$ in square TLR. The problem with having two elements like this is to get good expressions on both faces. The horse has moved slightly, which helps give liveliness.

P.72 Fig 17.1. Flash on camera. 1/125 second (fastest setting for flash) at f16.

P.72 Fig 17.2. Changed to 1/30 second at f11, flash diffused and reduced to quarter power with small piece of tracing paper.

P.73 Fig 17.6. Vital not to 'burn out' texture of snow. Exposure read off snow surface alone, then lens stopped down one stop.

P.73 Fig 17.9. Shot with standard lens on extension tube. 1/60 second at f16, on 200 ISO film. Focused for window reflection.

P.74 Fig 17.10. Curved wallpaper used as background. Lit with a single spotlight. Large white reflector on left. 1/30 second at f5.6. Camera on a tripod.

P.74 Fig 17.11. A selection of items from a boy's pocket, photographed on his desk, using overcast daylight from a (rear) window plus large white reflectors either side of the camera. General overall reading $\frac{1}{2}$ second at f16. Extension ring, tripod and cable release were used.

P.75 Figure 17.12. Spotlit from above, rear, plus a flood on the left. This flood was positioned so low it only illuminated the egg. A large white reflector board was held below and to the right of the lens. 1 second at f22, 125 ISO film.

P.82 Fig 20.1. Fairground at late dusk. Exposure read off white card (page 147). 2 seconds at f8, using tripod.

P.83 Fig 20.3. Clear, still moonless night. $1\frac{1}{2}$ hours at f16, worked out from test exposures. 125 ISO film. Streaks encircle the Pole Star.

P.83 Fig 20.4. Shot at night, panning, using the existing light on the roundabout, 1/60 second at f2. A compact direct vision viewfinder camera is the easiest type for panning.

P.84 Fig 20.6. This is much easier to do with a direct viewfinder or TLR camera – you don't lose the viewfinder image while the shutter is open. Include lights at varied distances, so the extent of movement differs throughout the picture.

P.85 Fig 20.8. Notice how the line becomes thicker and more 'burnt out' where the movement has slowed up (e.g. near the top of each stroke). At f16 give an exposure time as long as needed to complete the word – here it was 10 seconds. Taken in a completely blacked out studio, black background.

156

P.86 Fig 20.9. Car moving at speed along well lit road at night. Reading off road surface. Camera panned (too slowly) at 1/8 second at $f4$.

P.87 Fig 20.10. Exposure measured off ground, was 1/60 second at $f11$. Three exposures at 1/60 second were given, tilting camera sideways on its tripod by an equal amount each time. 2¼ in square TLR.

P.88 Fig 20.12. Important not to stop down excessively, or too much detail of items on water surface record too. 1/300 second at $f2.8$.

P.88 Figure 20.13. The children pressed their noses hard against square patterned glass. 1/60 second at $f5.6$.

P.93 Figure 22.2. Exposure read from the projected image on the hand (don't let the meter cast a shadow) ¼ second at $f4$, tungsten light film. To avoid subject movement provide some firm support for the wrist.

P.99 Fig 23.7. Two prints, see text. Exposure measured off the distant landscape and water, thus underexposing foreground.

P.112 Figs 26.9–17. Underexposed examples received ¼ of correct exposure; overexposed 4 times correct. Underdeveloped negatives had half correct development time; overdeveloped received twice correct time.

P.123 Fig 28.5. Photographed taking highlight and shadow meter readings from the dogs' faces only. 1/125 second at $f5.6$. 125 ISO film.

P.126 Figs 28.18 and 20. General exposure reading taken from the camera, pointing camera slightly downwards. No filter – sky overcast. 1/25 second at $f11$. On the print cottage was locally lightened with ferricyanide reducer (page 149).

P.127 Figs 28.22–3. Dog in kennel lit by overcast daylight through the removed roof, 1/250 second at $f4$.

P.129 Fig 28.30. A test strip showed that a 10 second exposure just resulted in a rich black when developed. 5 seconds exposure was therefore given, all the sweets moved around slightly, then another 5 seconds given.

P.132–3 Figs 29.6–13. Sequence edited down from 3 films (36 pictures 2¼ in square). The theme was planned in broad outline but then situations photographed as they happened. Humans were kept out of the way – picture 6 was shot later to complete the story. Picture 4 is a combination (cut-and-stick) of two prints, vertically joined. Unfortunately light kept varying from overcast to sunny. Exposure mostly 1/250 second at $f8$.

P.134–5 Fig 29.14. In laying out a picture essay often the most complicated pictures look better larger in size than simple ones. There are exceptions, e.g. where you want to give emphasis or impact to one special feature. Note how relationships can be used *within* pictures (the shop window models and passers-by) and *between* pictures (the crowded roofs and the crowded shoppers).

INDEX

Abstract compositions, 82–88
Advertising, 140–141
Albums, 135
Animals, 70–71, 142
  lenses, 34
Aperture, 10–11
  creative control, 24–27, 29
  enlargers, 123
  priority, 30
  SLR cameras, 15
Architecture, 66–67
  lenses, 34, 35
Assessment of work, 137
Autofocus, 10, 27
  faulty, 79
Automatic cameras
  aperture priority, 24–27
  blurring effects, 82–83
  exposure control, 29–30
  focus, 15
  light readings, 12–13
  panoramas, 98
  shutter priority, 21

B setting, 78
  double images, 94
  experimenting with, 82
Background, 11, 54
Bellows, 73, 107
Black and white, 18
  darkroom work, 108
  hand coloured, 96–97
  mood, 59
  seeing in, 48
Bleaching, 148–149
Blurring effects, 22–23
  painting with light, 84–86
  panning, 84
  steady camera and, 82–83
Boom lighting, 101
Bromide paper, 116
Burn out
  exposure problem, 29, 31
Burning in (printing in), 126–128, 129

Cable release, 22
Camera obscura, 6–8
Camera shake, 22, 30, 34, 79

Cameras
  compact, 11–13, 16
  larger formats, 144
  manual, 16, 30
  35 mm, 10–16
  single-lens reflex, 14–16, 25, 38
  twin-lens reflex, 144
  view, 144–145
Captions, 133
Changing bags, 109
Chemicals
  film processing, 108, 109–110
  printing, 115
  safety, 150
  toning and bleaching, 148–149
Children, 34, 62–63
Cityscapes, 66–67
Classes, 137
Close-up photography, 72–75
  attachments, 73
  camera shake, 72
  exposure readings, 146–147
  fill-in flash, 42
  film choice, 74
  half-lens, 90
  lenses, 14
Clubs, 137
Colour
  emphasis, 53
  by hand, 95, 96–97
  lighting equipment, 101, 102
  mood, 58–59
  processing, 108
  toning prints, 148–149
Colour film, 18
  balance, 103
  contact printing, 118
Communication
  information, 140–142
  photographic, 138–143
Compact cameras, 11–13, 16
  zoom lenses, 33
Compact Disk storage, 136
Composition see also Seeing
  emphasis, 49–54
  framing, 46, 52–53
  horizons, 68
  lines, 54
  pattern and shape, 55–57
  proportions, 46

Computers
    photographing screens, 107
Contact printing, 114–119
    equipment and chemicals, 114–116
    procedure, 116–118
Contact printing frame, 115–116
Contrast
    fill-in flash, 41
    film v eye, 47
    patterns, 56
    printing, 123–126
    studio lights, 105
    subject emphasis, 53
    texture, 61
Copying, 107
Criticism, 137

Darkrooms
    contact printing, 114–119
    enlargements, 120–129
    equipment, 108–109, 114–116, 120–121
    excluding light, 114
    film processing, 108–113
    ventilation, 114
Density, 111–112
Depth
    illusion, 48
    lines, 51–52
Depth-of-field
    camera choice, 11
    close-ups, 72
    compact cameras, 11
    maximum effect, 24–26
    minimum effect, 26–27
    preview, 25
    scale, 25–26, 27
Developer, 108, 109–110, 115, 127
Diaphragms see Aperture
Diffusion filters, 102, 150
Distorted images, 86
Documentaries
    sequences and essays, 131–134
    themes, 76
Dodging (shading), 126–128, 129
Double images, 92–94
    printing, 96
    projects, 94
Dry mounting, 131
Drying prints, 116, 130

Electrical equipment, 114–115
    safety, 150
Electronic circuits, 141
Electronic metering see Automatic cameras
Emotions as themes, 76
Emphasis, 49–54
    lighting, 106
    position, 52
    projects, 53–54
    tone or colour, 53

Emulsion, 8 see also Film
Enlargers, 9, 115, 116, 120–121
    focusing, 128–129
    safety, 150
Enlarging, 120–129
    film choice, 17
    test prints, 121–123
Equipment see Cameras; Darkrooms;
    Lighting
Errors
    assessing lab results, 78–81
Etiquette
    asking permission to photograph, 65
Evaluating photographs, 137
Experimental images
    distortions, 86
    movement and abstraction, 82–88
Exposure
    combined, 92–94
    creative control, 28–32
    enlargers, 123
    faults, 78–79
    filters, 91
    long, 22
    printing, 116
    tricky situations, 31–32
Extension rings and tubes, 73, 107

F-numbers, 11, 24, 26
Farmer's Reducer, 148, 149
Fibre-based paper, 118
Filing and storage, 135–136
Fill-in flash, 40–41
Film, 17–19, 103
    black and white, 18
    colour, 18
    expiry, 18
    faults in processing, 111–113
    faulty exposure, 124–125
    filing and storage, 110, 135–136
    hairs, 79
    image failure, 78–79
    loading and unloading, 11, 12–13, 17
    processing, 108–113
    roll and sheet, 144–145
Film processing
    faulty, 124–125
Film speed, 17–18
    close-up photography, 74
    compact cameras and, 12
    exposure control, 29
    setting camera, 18
Filters, 89, 91
    black and white, 48
    colour balancing, 103
    colour correction, 18
    contrast for printing, 120
Fisheye lens, 35, 37
Fixing solution, 108, 110, 115, 116, 127
Flare, 79

159

Flash
  animals, 70
  bad effects of, 38–39
  creative control, 38–44
  distances, 38, 40–41
  double images, 94
  fill-in, 40–41
  guide number, 38
  identifying errors, 79
  off-camera, 41–44
  open technique, 42, 44
  red eye, 39
  shutter speed, 38
  SLR cameras, 15
  stroboscopic effect, 44
  studio equipment, 102
Floodlights, 101, 102
Focus, 8
  autofocus, 10, 15, 27
  camera type, 10
  close-up, 72–74
  enlargers, 128–129
  selective, 27
Fogging, 78, 127
Foreground, 11, 52–53, 54
Frames, 130–131
Framing (composition), 46, 52–53
Freezing action, 20–21
Function of a photograph, 137

Grain, 17–18, 74
Guide number, 38

Hand tinting, 95
Health and Safety, 150
High key light, 59
Highlights, 29
Hockney, David, 99–100
Horizons, 68
Hot shoe, 41
Hypo, 108

Ilford, XP2, 18
Incident light, 146
ISO (International Standards Organization),
  17–18

Joiners, 99–100

Klee, Paul, 82

Laboratory processing
  identifying faults, 78–81
Landscapes, 66–69
  colour and mood, 58–59
  exposure, 30
  filters, 91
  lenses, 34, 35
  weather, 68

Lenses, 7–8, 10
  abberations, 8
  attachments, 89–91
  close-up, 14, 72
  effect of focal length, 33–37
  enlarging, 120
  fisheye, 35, 37
  flare, 79
  interchangeable, 14, 33–34
  macro, 73, 74
  perspective control, 34
  SLR systems, 14
  telephoto, 22, 30, 33, 34, 63, 70
  wide angle, 33, 35
  zoom, 33, 34, 37, 74
Light
  basis of photography, 6–7
  high and low key mood, 59
  painting with, 84–86
Light readings, 146–147
  automatic, 12–13, 15–16
  centre-weighted, 31–32
  creative exposure, 29
  faulty, 79
  freezing action, 21
  manual cameras, 14–15
  spot, 31–32
  tricky situations, 31–32
Lighting
  basic equipment, 101–102
  controlling, 103–107
  copying, 107
  fill-in, 105
  film speed, 17
  more than one source, 106
  patterns, 56
  people, 63
  safety, 150
  texture, 61
Lines, 51–52, 54
  architecture, 66–67
  horizons, 68
Low key light, 59

Macro focus, 73
Medical photography, 141
Metering see Light Readings
Microscopic photography, 14, 142
Modelling lamps, 102
Montages, 95–96
Mood, 53
  colour and, 58–59
  lighting, 106
Mosaics, 99–100
Motordrive
  panoramas, 98
Movement
  experimental images, 82–88
Multi-mode functioning, 15, 16
Multigrade paper, 116, 120, 121, 123–126;
  see also Contrast
  filters, 120
Multiple image filters, 90

Narrative themes, 76
Negatives, 9; *see also* Film
Neutral density filter, 91
Newspapers, 138–139
Night photography, 23, 68, 86

Overdevelopment, 112, 113
Overexposure, 29–29, 112, 113

Painting with light, 84–86
Panning, 21
Panoramas, 95, 97–98
Paper (photographic), 9
  multigrade, 120, 123–126
  types, 116, 118
Parallax error, 12, 14, 79, 144
Pattern and shape, 55–57; *see also*
  Experimental images
Perspective control, 34, 35–37
Photo-CDs, 136
Photo-tint dyes, 97
Photograms, 118, 129
Photojournalism, 138–139
Physiogram patterns, 88
Places, 66–69
  documentary themes, 76
Portraits and people, 62–65
  asking permission, 65
  children, 34, 62–63
  groups, 63–64
  lenses and lighting, 63
  lighting, 105
  strangers, 65
  telephoto lenses, 34
  themes, 76
Presentation, 130–136
  albums, 135
  filing and storage, 135–136
  mounting prints, 130–131
  sequences and essays, 131–134
Printing, 9
  contacts, 114–119
  drying, 130
  enlargement, 120–129
  faults, 127
  from faulty negatives, 112, 113
  printing in and shading, 126–128, 129
  unusual effects, 129
Printing in, 126–128, 129
Prints
  drying, 116
  experimental, 95–100
  identifying faults, 78, 79
  mounting, 130–131
  sequences and essays, 131–134
  toning and bleaching, 148–149
Processing film, 108–113
  equipment, 108–109
  faults, 111–113, 124–125
  lab corrections, 32
Projected double images, 92–93

Projects
  animals, 71
  close-ups, 74
  double images, 94
  emphasis, 53–54
  movement and abstraction, 87–88
  pattern and shape, 57
  places, 69
  printing experiments, 100
  seeing, 48–49
  texture, 61
Proportions, 46

Red eye, 39, 70
Reflector boards, 102
Resin-coated (RC) paper, 116, 118
Roll film, 144

Safety, 150
Sandwiching slides, 92
Scientific and technical photogrpahy, 141–142
Seeing, 45–49
  in black and white, 48
  choosing the moment, 48
  depth, 48
  framing, 46
  projects, 48–49
  selection, 47
Sepia tone, 148–149
Shading prints, 126–128, 129
Sharpness
  aperture, 24–26
Sheet film, 144–145
Shutters
  aperture and, 24
  B setting, 22, 44
  blurring effects, 29
  creative controls, 20–23
  fixed, 11–12, 16
  35 mm camera, 10
  SLR cameras, 15
Shutter
  identifying errors, 78
Silhouettes, 56
Single-lens-reflex (SLR) cameras, 14–16
  aperture, 25
  close-up attachments, 73
  flash and, 38
Slides, 18
  copying, 107
  identifying faults, 78, 79
  sandwiching, 92
  storage, 135–136
SLR *see* Single-lens-reflex cameras
Sport
  exposure, 30
  freezing action, 20–21
  lenses, 34
Spotlights, 101, 102, 106
Spray adhesive, 130
Star tracks, 83

Starburst filters, 90
Steadiness, 22, 30, 34, 79
  tripods, 22, 24, 74, 103
Still life, 74
Stop bath, 110
Stops *see* Aperture; F-numbers
Strobe effect, 44
Structure, 137
  themes based on, 76
Studios
  setting up, 101–102
Sunlight
  studio and, 106–107

Technical phtography, 141–142
Technical quality, 137
Telephoto lenses, 33
  animals, 70
  best uses of, 34
  camera shake, 22, 30, 34
  people, 63
Telescopes, 14
Television
  photographing screens, 107
Texture
  oblique flash, 42
  projects, 61
  studio lighting, 105
Themes, 76–77
  sequences and essays, 131–134
Tone
  emphasis, 53
  tonal interchange, 53
Toning, 148–149

Transparencies *see* Slides
Travel photography, 66–67
Trays, 115
Tripods, 22, 24; *see also* Steadiness
  close-ups, 74
  studio work, 103
  see also Camera shake
Twin Lens Reflex cameras, 144

Underdevelopment, 111–113
Underexposure, 28, 111–113

View Cameras, 144–145
Viewfinders, 10, 11
  compact cameras, 12

Watercolours, 97
Weather, 67–68
Wetting agent, 110
Wide angle lenses, 33
  best uses for, 35
Wind-on, 11
Window mats, 130

X-rays, 141

Zoom lenses, 33, 74
  compact cameras, 13
  effects, 37
  SLR cameras, 34